Praise for

Speak Up for a Child:

Reflections of a Lifelong Teacher

In *Speak Up for a Child*, Jeanne Strong has elegantly captured her lifelong work on behalf of the children of the world. We share a commitment to undoing injustice, a belief in the importance of educational leadership, a passion for children and learners of all ages, and the belief that we do indeed "teach who we are." By telling her story, Jeanne invites others who also work on behalf of children, to reflect on how their own personal and professional identities can form or deform the lives of children. She inspires me to listen more deeply to myself and to the voices of the many whose lives I touch.

—John Morefield, Educational Consultant

Jeanne Strong's memoir is an alive, inspiring testament to the power of story and to what happens when we follow our calling, reflecting deeply upon the journey every step of the way. This book's tender wisdom will provide inspiration and practical support to anyone passionate about education, learning and empowering the next generation. The core principles derived from Jeanne's lifelong commitment to children can be applied anywhere in our world—a world so in need of a revolution in how we engage and nurture the potential of young people everywhere.

—Charlie Murphy, CEO, Partners for Youth
Empowerment (PYE Global)

In the tradition of Sylvia Ashton Warner, George Dennison, and Vivian Paley, Jeanne Strong weaves the compelling story of her lifetime in teaching, beginning with harrowing stories of her childhood in China through finding a post-retirement calling to serve students and teachers in a village in Uganda. With her telling, she calls each of us to contribute to the well-being of children.

—Terry Chadsey, Executive Director
Center for Courage & Renewal

I am at a loss to put into words what I want to say, for Jeanne has captured the essence of teaching and learning and indeed what it means to be human. Her innate ability to perceive children for who they are and her reflection on her own experiences as a child surface the wondrous gifts she brings to the world of teaching and learning. She understands that the complexity of being a child is no less profound than that of any adult. Her writing speaks eloquently to the knowledge that our physical presence and body language speaks much louder than any words we may utter. Jeanne has put into words those intangible teacher qualities that create the deep partnership between a teacher and student—so necessary for magic to occur for all learners. Her stories make this a must-read for any educator, and most especially essential for new teachers.

—Anita Garcia Morales, Educator and
Community Activist

This book is built on the power of story. Jeanne uses personal narrative to reflect on her own values and how they have informed her practice as a teacher. In the process she invites us to remember our own particular stories as a way to reconnect with the values underlying who we are as teachers and learners. At a time when teachers are buffeted by requirements that may have little to do with children and their learning, this book can help us remember why we went into teaching in the first place.

As a teacher of both adults and children there have always been times of discouragement. At these moments, I often turn to a favorite book to remind myself of the importance of paying attention to the children and relationships that form the core of teaching and learning. *Speak Up for a Child* will become one of these anchor books for me.

—Nancy Place, Associate Director and Professor,
University of Washington, Bothell

In my role as advocate for youth in foster care, I found this book thought provoking and at the same time a confirmation of my own beliefs about children and their needs. Last week I witnessed an example of what Jeanne writes about.

A fourteen-year-old boy, neglected and at times abandoned by his mother, has spent the last twenty-four months in foster care. His father was recently released from prison after serving a sentence for brutally beating the boy's mother. The boy moved from foster home to foster home because he couldn't adjust to the different families' structures. Finally, he arrived in a home with a foster mother who met him with an open heart. She provided him a place of peace where he could begin to heal.

But unable to trust that this could really be a woman who was willing to care for him indefinitely, he asked to be moved to another home. His care team met with him. Also invited to the table were his school coach and counselor, his foster mother, and family friends whose home the boy visited frequently. The group honored his desire to move, and asked him to explain what he was hoping for in the next home so that a better match could be made.

He began to list features he had experienced in his current home, although wisely, no one pointed that out. Instead, his coach spoke first, and told the boy how much he had seen him grow in the months he'd known him. He noted increased self-confidence, which led to increased athletic skills. Then he told the boy how much he appreciated him as a person, and wished they could have an ongoing relationship, even after high school. Suddenly, the other people from his community chimed in with similar comments. The boy laughed, and said he realized he was probably where he needed to be.

In the trial to terminate his mother's parental rights, the boy told the judge he had finally come to a home that was stable, where he felt loved and safe. He said he loved his school. He said he couldn't envision ever going back to live with his mother, although he hoped they could still keep in touch. In the next few months, he will be adopted by the foster mother who honors him for who he is, and has given him the safety and security he needs to begin to imagine a future that includes college and the pursuit of an engineering degree. He has experienced the power of a caring community.

This real-life story serves to underscore the critical importance of Jeanne Strong's message about the need to value, respect and honor children. As adults, we are reminded to be kind and careful stewards of this invaluable human treasure.

—*Carla Grau-Egerton, CASA Program Manager*

Jeanne reminds us all, in *Speak Up for a Child* that children are not little objects, but very real human beings making sense of the world in very reasonable ways. When we, as adults, (literally) look over their heads, we miss important information and miss connecting with them. Jeanne not only listens deeply to but also advocates for children in a way that supports them, that helps them sense their own value and empowers them to be the full human beings that they can be. We can all learn from her example.

—*Jody McVittie, MD, Certified Positive Discipline Lead Trainer*

Speak Up for a Child

Speak Up for a Child

Reflections of a Lifelong Teacher

Jeanne R. Strong

Abiding Nowhere Press
Greenbank, Washington

Published by Abiding Nowhere Press
Printed in the USA
www.abidingnowhere.com

ISBN - 978-0-9854967-5-3 (Abiding Nowhere Press)

Credits

Cover design by Sandra Welch
Cover photo by Nik Strong-Cvetich
Author photo by Ken Driese

The phrase *Speak Up for a Child* has been used by various
CASA programs around the nation.

Permissions

"The Way It Is," by William Stafford, is from *The Way It Is: New &
Selected Poems* (Graywolf Press, 1998) Reprinted here by permission of
The Estate of William Stafford.

"My Head Is Full of Children," used by permission of the artist Kiki
Suarez (Irene de Suarez Oberstenfeld)

*For obvious reasons the names in these stories have been changed, with
the exception of my sons and my Ugandan friend Jane, who all gave
their permission to be identified.*

To the children, near and far, who have captured my heart

Table of Contents

Introduction

If we are to reach real peace in the world,
we shall have to begin with the children.
—Mahatma Gandhi

The very first words I remember knowing how to read were **US GO HOME**, spray-painted on the Paris airport wall. It was September of 1951, just a month shy of my sixth birthday. "Why do they want *us* to go home? We just got here . . ." I asked my mother. Having been displaced a number of times in my young life, I really had little idea of where home was. I don't remember what my mother told me, except to explain that *us* meant the U.S., and that some people, six years after the end of World War II, were angered by the continued presence of American troops.

What does *war* mean in the mind of a five-year-old? What does GO HOME mean to a five-year-old with little experience of home? Where is home? What is the U.S.? What is *us*? Can *us* be larger than U.S.? These are still questions I wonder about.

Fifty years later, almost to the day, on September 11, 2001, Sameh, age five, came to me across the playground. "We Muslims are not all like that, you know." He makes sure that I know him, that I see him, this Tunisian boy who wants to feel at home in the U.S.

Julie at age six, when several visitors to our classroom ask why the children are all reading different books, looks up with her calm and earnest eyes and replies, "We are all different people."

I show Mikeh pictures of children in my school in the U.S. "Why are some brown?" he wants to know. We talk of immigration, of slavery, he who has never seen a city, a river, an ocean, never been beyond the rolling hills of his remote Ugandan village. "If I go to A-me-ri-ka, will my skin turn white?" he asks.

Children, for as long as I can remember, have played a central role in my life. I am fascinated with their language, curious about their feelings and about how they understand and make sense of the world and their place in it.

Who speaks up for the children of the world who, like Sameh, want to be seen? Who speaks up for the children of the world whose curiosity, like Mikeh's, has nowhere to turn? My life as a teacher has been about speaking up for children, or rather encouraging them to find their own voice, as I help them to make sense of the world.

Can we envision a world where we can truly become *us*? *Us* as citizens of the world, *us* as Julie understood how we can all be different, *us* as recognition that we are all in this together, regardless of where we come from and the circumstances of our birth? How do I help children understand, accept, and embrace differences—differences across race, culture, class, language, and beliefs? That is truly the basis for peace. As Gandhi said, "We shall have to start with the children."

How did I come to embrace this perspective?

My family's story, my personal story, and the stories of the children I have taught have all contributed. We are shaped by life's unfolding. And in this unfolding there has been, for me, a thread.

The poet William Stafford, in *The Way It Is*,[1] writes:

> *There is a thread you follow. It goes among*
> *things that change. But it doesn't change.*
> *People wonder about what you are pursuing.*
> *You have to explain about the thread.*
> *But it is hard for others to see.*
> *While you hold it you can't get lost.*
> *Tragedies happen; people get hurt*
> *or die; and you suffer and get old.*
> *Nothing you do can stop time's unfolding.*
> *You don't ever let go of the thread.*

---

1. William Stafford, *The Way It Is* (Saint Paul, MN: Graywolf Press, 1993), 42.

The older I get, the more I realize my life has been guided by an invisible thread, the strength of which has been tested over and over. As John Sanford says, "Life's supreme achievement may be to see the thread that connects together the events, the dreams, and relationships that have made up the fabric of our existence."[2]

In this book I tease out that thread, not only the thread of my own life and how it has shaped the fabric of the teacher I have become, but how my thread is rooted and woven into the threads of previous generations in my family. Perhaps it may even provide some warp for the tapestries of generations to come. I now understand that this thread has permeated all that I have done in my life. When I was twelve I decided that when I grew up I wanted to teach kindergarten in Africa. Twenty years later I was teaching a yearlong course at The Evergreen State College titled *Third World Focus on Early Childhood Development,* and thirty-five years after that I found myself building an Early Learning Center in East Africa, where kindergartners joyfully learn. Only recently have I connected all those dots, but that invisible thread was there all along.

Speak Up for a Child is the thread, with its many twists and turns, that I have followed all my life, perhaps from a deep longing for someone to speak up for my five-year-old self. For me, this thread, *Speak Up for a Child* invites me to look

2. John Sanford, from *Healing and Wholeness* in Marv and Nancy Giles, *An Almanac for the Soul* (Healdsburg, CA: Iona Center, 2008), 60.

at how my life is part of a bigger picture; how I as a teacher try to bring all of who I am to the classroom, and how my responses to my family's values are reflected in all that I do. I am grateful to the many guides along the way, many of them children, who have helped me hold on to my own thread.

> *My story is important not because it is mine . . . but because if I tell it anything like right, the chances are you will recognize that in many ways it is yours . . .*[3]

I have learned to pay attention to where I'm from, to my roots, and to *stop, look,* and *listen* to what is before me. We are each shaped by the fabric of our cultural and familial backgrounds, and by the experiences we encounter along the way. Whether you are a teacher, a therapist, a social worker, or anyone else working with children and their families, this book is an invitation to look more closely at what has shaped your life and work.

---

3. Frederick Buechner, *Telling Secrets* (New York, NY: HarperCollins, 1991), 17.

Speak Up for a Child

Chapter One

We Teach Who We Are

Who is the self that teaches?[4]

Each of us has a story. Each of us is many stories. My story, regardless of how dramatic or mundane, has shaped me, just as we are each shaped by our stories. The important thing is to know and acknowledge how my story has shaped my perceptions, my values, for as Parker Palmer writes in *The Courage to Teach*, "We teach who we are."[5] We often talk, says Dr. Palmer, of what to teach, or how to teach, or even sometimes philosophically about why we teach, but "seldom, if ever, do we ask the 'who' question—who is the self that teaches? How does the quality of my selfhood form —or deform—the way I relate to my students, my subject,

---

4. Parker J. Palmer, *The Courage to Teach* (San Francisco, CA: Jossey-Bass, 1997), 4.

5. Ibid., 2.

my colleagues, my world?"[6] Self-knowledge becomes the foundation of good teaching, because if I am effective, who *I am* will be ever-present in my teaching. This is true of anyone working in service of others. It is my presence, all of who I am, that will allow me to connect with children, to build the relationships that enable learning. Teaching is first about building relationships.

A number of years ago, I was sitting with some colleagues in a nearly empty restaurant for an early dinner, and in another corner sat a family. I recognized Peter first, then his older brother, Evan, and his younger sister, Jessie. I had taught all three of them some twelve years earlier. The waitress came over to our table and asked which one of us was a teacher.

"All of us," I replied.

"Which one of you taught the children of that family?" I owned up. "What did you teach them?" the waitress wanted to know.

"Why don't you ask them?"

She came back a short time later with our order, and I asked what their response had been. "They said you taught them *life*." It still makes me smile.

こう こう こう

---

6. Ibid., 4.

Where I'm From

My story is important not because it is mine . . . but because if I tell it anything like right, the chances are you will recognize that in many ways it is yours. Maybe nothing is more important than that we keep track . . . of these stories of who we are and where we have come from and the people we have met along the way because it is precisely through these stories in all their particularity . . . that our spirit makes itself known to us most powerfully and personally . . .[7]

In my work with teachers, I frequently start the school year or the workshop with an activity originally designed by Linda Christiansen in *Reading, Writing, and Rising Up*, called "Where I'm From: Inviting Students' Lives Into the Classroom."[8] I invite my students to paint a picture of their lives with words. I use my own story as a model:

---

7. Frederick Buechner, *Telling Secrets,* 17.

8. Linda Christiansen, *Reading, Writing and Rising Up: Teaching about Social Justice and the Power of the Written Word* (A Rethinking School Publication, 2003), 18.

Where I'm From . . .

I'm from buckets of scalding bathwater and steep hills to climb and making cloud pictures in the sky . . . from shots and soldiers and baobao *me, fleeing in the dark of night.*

I'm from "Why do we have to move again?" and all-day kick the can, and spying on Mom's lemon meringue pie from the top branch of my favorite tree . . . from marble games in six languages. Alors, tu viens maintenant? Ou quoi? *I'm from chopsticks and melting cheese and bread with chocolate, and from the dreaded metronome that kept time faster than me.*

I'm from pipe tobacco and Nana's silently pursed and frowning lips, though she never admonished me. I'm from Grandpa's chair and growing up quick because he knew I could . . . from watching and wondering, listening and learning, new languages, new customs, new cultures, new faces.

I'm from brothers and sons, from kids, my teachers: David and Marcolo, Jose and Orrin, Johanna and Yvette, Meron and Mar'Jon . . . from "I can" to "who needs teachers?"

I'm from challenges and questioning, pushing my thinking and heart together. I'm from those who inspired me to go beyond, to think big, to see the world from all sides, inside and out. I'm from SPIRIT carved in rock, from "know you are an old soul . . ." though we never spoke of it.

I'm from "make the world a better place . . ." I'm from big shoes to fill and making my own footprints.

I come from a family of peacemakers, though we never called it that. Those "big shoes to fill" have clearly been for me both an inspiration and a challenge. My parents, shortly after they were married, went to China during World War II. After her release and repatriation from a Japanese internment camp in China in 1943, my mother, Kitty, wrote:

I now have an idea of what it is to live behind barbed wire, to be in prison, to be an enemy alien, one of the persecuted, the hated, the scorned. . . . I have been hungry and thirsty, and I know the all-absorbing power of these drives. . . . Unless the problems of the thousands of still-uprooted, wandering peoples are met by those who keep the peace, and some attempt is made to heal their wounds, it will be peace, but for a season.

My great-grandfather, Sydney Dix Strong, a congregational minister, lost his church during World War I for being a pacifist. In 1903 he and my great-grandmother, Ruth Maria, traveled across the Atlantic to the coast of West Africa, around the Cape of Good Hope and the Horn of Africa, visiting villages and missions all the way around the continent. She died at the end of that voyage.

His son, my grandfather, Tracy Strong, traveled throughout the Middle East in the early 1950s, trying to broker peace between Palestinians and the newly formed state of Israel. Sydney's daughter, my great-aunt, Anna Louise Strong, spent the last twenty years of her life as a journalist in China, witness to the Cultural Revolution.

My father's younger brother, Tracy Jr., also followed in the family's footsteps, working tirelessly during World War II behind the scenes in France and Germany in prisoners-of-war camps, sometimes helping Jews escape to freedom, traveling across borders under false papers, and endangering his life in his commitment to work for peace and justice.

My father, Robbins, loved to tell the story of a conversation his aunt Anna Louise had with Mao Tse Tung. Mao asked her to tell him in ten words or less the meaning of Christianity. She immediately responded, "Peace and justice for all." Mao's response still resonates with me through my father's account: "And what have you done about it?"

My father's life, as an ordained minister like his grandfather, was anchored in the Social Gospel of "peace and justice for all" and "what have you done about it?" My parents went to China first as missionaries, and then quickly switched to the YMCA when my father clearly felt he had no business telling others what to believe. He explained that, at that time, most missionaries' idea of "peace and justice for all" was confined to converting others to a narrow and Western view of the Gospel, rather than the essential Christian message of "love thy neighbor,"—*not* "smother thy neighbor."

When my son Nik was nine years old, he had a school assignment to talk to someone of his grandparents' generation about their remembrances of war. He wrote to my father, and promptly received the following response:

May 16, 1991

Dear Nik,

I have your letter asking me about my memories of wars. That is a big job because during my life there have been too many of them. All that I can do is pick out a few incidents.

The first war that I can remember is what is now called World War I, which lasted from 1914 to 1918. All that I can remember about it is that on the night that it ended I was awakened to hear the bells ringing for joy; I was then just a little younger than you. This is the best memory that I have of any war because it was the end of that war.

The next war in which I was involved was the war between Japan and China, which began in 1937 and which later became what is now called World War II, I was in China at that time. Just one memory of it, although I have many: The Japanese had already captured Peking where I was. One day I was traveling on a train going from Peking to Shansi province. The Japanese controlled the railroads but the Chinese guerillas were all around it in the countryside. I was in a train compartment sleeping. One of the other persons was a Japanese.

Suddenly the train stopped with a jerk. The lights went out and then bullets began to hit the side of the train. The Japanese in my compartment was very scared. I didn't know how to feel. I was worried that I might get hit, but then I was glad that the Chinese had been able to wreck a Japanese train. The Japanese guards on the train put a machine gun on the top of our car and started shooting out into the dark. This went on for several hours and all we could do was lie there. In the morning the shooting stopped and we went out. The Chinese had blown up a little bridge, and the locomotive went off the tracks. So too did the first two cars of the train. The engine drivers were killed. In the field outside was one Chinese farmer who had been shooting at the train. He was killed. We then walked with our bags across the place where the bridge was blown up and the Japanese had another train there, and we continued our trip.

Later, when Pearl Harbor was bombed by the Japanese on December 7, 1941, the USA became part of this war. I was still in China in the Japanese area and thus I became what is called an "enemy alien." However, for me it did not begin on December 7, but on December 8. (See if you can figure that out.)

The first we knew about it was when ten Japanese soldiers came to our house and made us understand that we could not leave the house; we didn't know why. They didn't talk any English or Chinese, but they had guns and made clear what we should do. It was only three days later when they let our cook go out to buy some food that he smuggled in a newspaper under the vegetables and we knew that we were in the war.

After about a year we were sent to an internment camp just as were the Japanese in the USA, even those Japanese who were American citizens. It was there in this camp that your uncle Tracy was born, so we always used to say that he was born a prisoner. Finally, in 1943 we were repatriated and exchanged for the Japanese in the USA. We took two boats, one from China to India—where the exchange took place —and the other from India to South Africa and then to South America and finally to New York. The trip took about two and a half months.

The next war I was involved in was a civil war, the one between the Nationalists in China and the Communists in China. This war had been going on and off for about twenty years. My first experience of it was back in 1937 when I was teaching at Oberlin in China. The Communists invaded the province where I was and got to about ten miles from our school. Most of the foreigners left, but I stayed around. All the students stood guard duty around the walls of the school at night but the Communists never got there and were finally driven out of the province.

When this war was coming to an end, I was in Nanking. On a Thursday night the Nationalists, whose capital was Nanking, ran away. So did all the police.

The Communists did not arrive until Saturday. So there were two days without any government. Some of the police who ran away threw their guns over the wall into our yard along with their ammunition. We didn't know what to do about it and finally threw them into a septic tank in our backyard. Our neighbors got some guns from the police station but they didn't know how to use them; they were shooting them off in all directions and the bullets were hitting our wall. We had to keep your mother in the house.

Some days later after the Communists had taken over the city, your mother went back to school. She was then a small girl. The Nationalists sent over some airplanes to bomb the city and so the people at the school decided to send the kids home. They put her in a rickshaw, and she rode through the bombardment. Luckily, no bomb hit her. Otherwise, I do not know where you would be today.

I hope you never have to be in a war because I can assure you that they are not nice. It is one thing to study them but another to be in one. Then people suffer. And wars leave more problems than they solve . . .

Love, Grandpa

This is the family into which I was born. A family with a deep and abiding faith in the sanctity and goodness of all humankind; a tenacity of spirit, even in the face of seemingly insurmountable odds; an insatiable curiosity about the world and its diversity; a commitment to peace and to making the world a better place for all; a belief in the interconnectedness of us all; the courage to stand up to injustice; and a wisdom that comes from living with grace. High standards, to say the least. I was taught that if I don't hold myself to expecting and honoring the best in people, I have done them a disservice by diminishing my belief in them.

æ æ æ

Lessons from Childhood

There is a thread you follow, it goes among things that change, but it doesn't change . . .
—William Stafford

My family's stories have helped to shape who I have become as a teacher: *"We teach who we are . . ."* as Parker Palmer writes. My family's values form my foundational threads, the warp of the tapestry of my life. Those threads are interwoven with the weft of my own life experiences. As Frederick Buechner reminds us: "My story is important not because it is mine. . . but because if I tell it anything like right, the chances are you will recognize that in many ways it is yours."

My own experiences, both early and current, continue to shape and strengthen the fabric of my life. My questions are also universal questions of childhood and humankind:

- Who is there for me?
- Will I be safe and cared for?
- Where do I belong?
- What is my place in the world?
- Am I good enough?

- Who believes in me?
- How do I treat others?

ॐ   ॐ   ॐ

Who is there for me?

My earliest years were spent in wartime China, moving, constantly moving, and sometimes fleeing with only what we could carry. I can still hear the clatter of hooves on the cobblestones of our courtyard, the mounted soldiers shouting, guns going off, grenades being thrown, the sound of shots everywhere. My first word in Chinese was *"Sha!"*[9] mimicking the Kuomintang soldiers running by the wall of our compound. My mother was alarmed, unable to project the lasting effects or protect her young children from witnessing daily scenes of violence.

We took off one day, like any other day in our rickshaw, my older brother Tracy and me: he in his little visor hat with padded earflaps, and me, in my quilted jacket and pants, dark blue with a faint whitish flower pattern, to go to school. My teacher, Miss Shu, greeted me at the door. It was a sunny day, though crisp and cold like most Nanking winters. We sang a greeting and counted each child. From playing with our neighbor Jung Chan, I had become quite the Chinese chatterbox. "Let the brush do the painting," said

---

9. Chinese for "kill!"

Miss Shu, as she watched my frustration with trying to make my picture look just so.

I was in the middle of letting my brush do whatever it wanted when my father was suddenly standing there. He felt taller than his lean six-foot-three-inch frame. "Come," he said, "we need to go."

"No," I cried, "I am not finished painting; I don't want to go."

He picked me up and carried me out to the open jeep where my brother was already sitting. As he got behind the wheel, a plane flew overhead. I heard a loud explosion just beyond my school. Stones and dust scattered. My father drove fast and my body froze, not knowing if I should duck as another plane dropping bombs flew overhead. My whole body was rigid with fear, though it was such a familiar feeling; it felt like I was wrapped in a self-created rigid shell, impenetrable, but one that didn't allow much freedom of movement. More bombs fell, but farther away, and my father raced on. We were suddenly at the gate of our compound. Our cook whisked me inside, scooping me up and carrying me into the house.

∿   ∿   ∿

In 1950, after living for a year under the Communist regime, my father felt that our presence was becoming a handicap and an embarrassment to his Chinese colleagues, and he decided to move us to Korea. Our stay was short-lived, but one filled with more violence, as the Korean War broke out. My mother wrote, after we had safely reached Japan:

Yes, it was just a week ago . . . on Saturday we moved into the freshly redecorated side of the duplex in Seoul – walls re-tinted, kitchen retiled, floors waxed. It was nice, and we worked hard getting it that way. Sunday afternoon at church we heard the news there was border activity going on. This was the first word we had heard. Having just come from Nanking in Communist China, we didn't feel worried, only amused at these people who got panicky at the word "Communist."

After supper, life was made grim by having Johnnie, then eighteen months old, back up and sit into a pail of near boiling bath water. (I hardly can remember it without feeling ill.) The poor little fellow was so burned that he was beyond screaming. I had enough presence of mind to empty a pound of baking soda into a dishpan and to simply swaddle him in clean diaper packs of warm soda solution for the rest of the night. As it was he came out with a raw line of blistered flesh where the rim of the pail caught him across the back . . .

Family lore would have it that I pushed my little brother, Johnnie, into the scalding water. My recollection is that, having emerged from my tepid bath, cooled after my older brother's bath, I padded, shivering and wrapped in a towel, down the narrow hall and passed my little brother just as he toddled toward the bathroom, past the pail of boiling water heated on the wood-burning stove. He stepped back to let me by, and sat right in the pail. Perhaps the need for family lore around this event was fueled by the events that followed . . .

At about 1:30 a.m. we were awakened from the troubled sleep we had finally gotten into after getting Johnnie to bed, by someone calling from the front lawn. It was Frank of USIS[10] who had been sent to call on those of us not on the State Department phone system—ordering immediate evacuation.

We were told to assemble by 3:00 a.m. It was very hard for us to believe it was necessary for us to pay attention—after China—but Rob did get out the jeep and drive down to the Embassy while I stayed in bed. He came back fast! Having seen the ambassador himself, with the word that the Reds were ten miles out of the city, and that the kids and I—at least—had to go at once.

Well, unbelieving, I threw clothes into a couple of suitcases, gently woke the kids and bandaged Johnnie's backside, and we piled into the jeep to go to where we were to assemble—well past 4:00 a.m. The bus had already left!

We drove like demons out to one of the military residence areas—no bus, no people—and then rushing down the road toward the airport, we caught up with a U.S. Army bus, which we flagged, and me and the kids piled in with a few already-present late-goers— and left Rob and the jeep by the side of the road.

---

10. USIS: United States Information Service.

The bus drove us like mad down the road to the port city, where we were whisked onto a Norwegian freighter with cabin space for twelve people, with the other 685 women and kids who had been rounded up. And we set sail for Tokyo before I had even made up my mind to go!

I still have vivid memories, from age four and a half, of those events: the chaos, the confusion, the fear I drank in from my parents. Sandwiched between two brothers: one self-possessed, confident, proudly carrying a suitcase with all his six-year-old muscles, his head held high; and the other barely a toddler with a scalded bottom, clinging to my mother's neck. I, who was too little to carry much, became invisible—I wanted only a hand to hold, but there were none. "*Baobao* me," I cried, Chinese for "hold me, carry me, hug me." Unseen, unheard, my anxiety over watching my father's face recede was, without a doubt, mirrored in my mother's body language. Would we ever see my father again?

ৡ   ৡ   ৡ

The effects of violence, to the body or to the soul, wound in deeper ways than we know. My early experiences of hearing gunfire, of watching soldiers on horseback in our compound, of playing with a live grenade because we didn't know any better, were etched deep in me. As a four-year-old I assumed this was "normal" life. Later when we had temporarily moved to a suburban New Jersey neighborhood,

I could never figure out why no one paid any attention to the daily air-raid sirens, which always sent me running into the house in a panic. I knew what that sound meant: planes coming soon to drop bombs.

As an adult I became aware of just how deep my somatic memory was. We were visiting some acquaintances in the Okanogan Valley in north central Washington on the opening weekend of deer-hunting season. In anticipation, several of the men were cleaning their rifles, preparing for the next day's pursuit, when standing not five feet from me, Fred fired off a test round. I nearly jumped out of my skin, my heart pounding. My early physical memories of gun violence came flooding back. Just the other day, a low-flying plane rumbled overhead. I realized I held my body braced in anticipation of gunfire or an explosion. Somatic memory runs deeper than conscious memory.

I carry in my cells a reaction to physical violence, and by extension violence to the psyche, somewhere deep in my solar plexus, with my shoulders standing guard, a state of hypervigilance where words don't penetrate, for the cerebral cortex has shut down. Is that why I have over the years identified with children whose lives have been affected by physical or emotional violence, who don't always know if they will be safe or who will be there for them? We continually have to ask ourselves how our early experiences affect our outlook.

         ૐ   ૐ   ૐ

Will I be safe and cared for?

After our abrupt departure from Korea, we lived briefly in Japan. Another incident of violence, firmly etched in my mind, took place in what we had hoped would become our "permanent" home. An angry and quite drunk Japanese man arrived at our house, yelling obscenities about American imperialists, trying to get into our house. He climbed up on my mother's window box, trampling her newly planted petunias, and pounding on the window. My father whisked us away from the window to a room upstairs. The man then climbed onto the roof to try to get in through an attic window. We were herded back downstairs. My father held a baseball bat.

This went on for quite some time, and in the end, much to my father's shame, he called the U.S. military police, as he didn't speak any Japanese to call the local police. The lesson I remember from witnessing him call in the police was his shame in resorting to his defacto power and imperialistic privilege. When he told the story, it was not about the safety of his family, but about his regret over solving a problem by resorting to the "might of white," only reinforcing the truth in the obscenities the drunk was hurling at us.

By then the fear, a physical rigidity in the face of violence, had become habitual in my four-year-old body. But this time it was overlaid by another fear—the fear that my father would also turn to violence by clubbing this angry man who was threatening our family.

For any child, physical safety is critical to developing self-confidence and competence. Given the chaos of my early years, my sense of confidence and competence, of having a place in the world, of belonging, was a long time in coming.

❧   ❧   ❧

Where do I belong?

Our stay in Tokyo was equally short-lived. Though I had hoped for a permanent home, it was not to be. After abruptly leaving Japan, we spent time with family back in the United States. I remember my fifth birthday. What was significant about that particular birthday is that my grandmother decided I no longer needed to be clad in my brother's drab, mismatched hand-me-downs, or in the shorts my mother had fashioned from rough Chinese sackcloth. It was the first time I had met my mother's mother and she strongly felt I needed to know I was a girl. For my birthday she gave me my first dress—a red plaid dress with a white collar, and a gold ring with my birthstone, a ruby. I now know my birthstone is really an opal, but I loved the ruby red, and I accepted what she told me. She showed me how to properly wear it on the fourth finger of my left hand. For many years, even long after I had outgrown the ring, the memory of it on my finger helped me remember right from left.

I also received my first pair of tie shoes—in China we wore cloth slip-ons, and in Korea and Japan, split-toed thongs with white-toed socks, not what one could call flip-flops, for they were of stiff woven grasses. So on my birthday, I learned to tie shoes, as well as tie my new dress behind my back while looking in the tall antique mirror in my grandmother's bedroom—with coaching from this rather formidable woman. Despite her stern demeanor and her ferocity about what was proper, she instilled in me a sense of pride and competence that I hadn't experienced before—not helping me, not doing for, but coaching.

∾ ∾ ∾

My budding sense of competence with my grandmother was undermined a few months later, when we moved to Paris, another new culture, and another new language.

My first day at La Petite École Nouvelle was one of revisiting invisibility. I was scared, though I had been taught never to show that. Six years old and I didn't speak the language. The other children were chatting with each other. The desks were arranged around three-quarters of the perimeter of a square, and each desk had a name tag on it. I wandered around looking for my name. At least I knew how to read my name, even if I couldn't speak. I saw a tag that had part of my name, but it didn't look like my name. Everyone had found his or her seat and still I was wandering.

My teacher, Anne-Marie, sensing my angst, showed me my seat, the only empty one, pointing to the word *JEANNE*. But I knew my name was spelled *JEAN*.

"*Ahh . . .*" she said, "*Mais c'est un nom de garçon . . .*"[11] And indeed, in French, *Jean* was not only a boy's name but also my brother John's name as well. From that day forward I became *Jeanne*.

This must have been a fairly progressive school, for we called our teacher by her first name. Anne-Marie, whom I came to love after a few months once I began to understand the language, was only trying to be helpful by giving me a gender-appropriate name. But her help left me feeling invisible, once again needing to take on a whole new identity. *Jean* for me was no more. I took great consolation in knowing I shared my name with Jeanne d'Arc, the martyred saint, and often asked my mother to take a detour past her statue, on the rue de Rivoli. We stayed in Paris for three years, and it began to feel like home.

So I was furious when my father announced that we were moving again—this time to Geneva: another new start, a new school, and new friends to make. Fortunately, the language stayed the same. My brothers and I effortlessly switched between French and English, sometimes in mid-sentence, and mercilessly ridiculed our mother, whose French accent was atrocious. We stayed in Geneva until I was almost seventeen when I went off to college. But finally, at

---

11. Translated "But that is a boy's name . . ."

age nine, for the first time in my life, I felt like I had a home.

∂   ∂   ∂

Am I good enough? Who believes in me?

Even if life was settled, and I already spoke the language used in school, I nevertheless was always "*la petite américaine*," never quite belonging. Even in my family, as a middle child and the only girl between two boys, I looked for ways to belong. I wanted so much to be seen, to be acknowledged. My perception was that to be seen you had to be older, bigger, and a boy. Family stories about my older brother splitting his head open on a balance beam, or contracting a drug-resistant staph infection, or reciting verbatim information that he read in the *Readers' Digest* or the dictionary spoke of his visibility. I, too, wanted to be seen, so I decided to surprise my mother by polishing the dining room table with floor wax. We waxed our hardwood floors every two weeks by hand—apply, wait, and buff. I had done it many times. We were never allowed to walk around barefoot, for the moisture of our feet would take the wax off. I never really believed that, but always complied.

No one was home. I carefully brought out the can of paste wax and the oily cloth. I put it on extra thick, perhaps as extra encouragement for my hope of recognition. I waited the required twenty minutes, admiring my work and eagerly anticipating my mother's joy. Slowly I polished, round and round, rubbing the wax into the wood, until it gleamed. I loved how the inlay lines of lighter wood deepened in tone. I buffed, starting at my father's end of the table and ending at my mother's, while I thought about our shared family meals—my favorite: my mother's Chinese food cooked at the table in a center hot pot; my least favorite: tomato aspic and spinach. I relived the joy of anticipating Sunday night waffles that my father tossed the length of the table. The waffles only fell on the floor if we tried to catch them. My father's pitching was always accurate.

It was almost time. I quickly put all my tools away and waited for the click of my mother's key in the door. I could hardly contain my excitement over the anticipation of her pleasure.

"What have you done?" exclaimed my mother. "Oh, no! What have you done to the dining room table?"

My enthusiasm dampened, confused by my mother's reaction. I wanted her approval. "I waxed it. I wanted to surprise you."

"No, no, we never wax the table. It has its own natural oils and we never, never, ever wax it," she admonished me.

I shrunk and had no words, for I had failed. I was only wanting to be seen, to be acknowledged. The table was fine; my wounded ego was not. I am sure my mother never knew how her words affected me or she might have softened her tone and acknowledged my attempts to be helpful. We don't always know how our words affect others, especially vulnerable children.

ॐ   ॐ   ॐ

How do I treat others?

Because of my father's work, we spent the summer months before I turned ten back in Paris. It was during that summer that I learned how others thought about differences between people. Ruby came to live with us because she needed a place to stay, and, in return, she helped with our family. I remember mostly her hair and her voice. Her hair was pulled back and held in a very short clump at the nape of her neck. It also seemed to stay in the shape she combed it, never blown about in the wind like mine. Her fingers were long, her cheekbones high. We sat listening to a record of Hans Christian Anderson, and she began to sing. I stopped listening to the record and stared at her, drawn in by her beautiful voice. Later that night when she was putting me to bed she sang again "Sometimes I feel like a motherless child . . ." Had she felt that way too? I wondered.

Ruby took me to my first piano lesson with Mr. Goldberg. After my lesson she and Mr. Goldberg talked for a long time, but I lost interest, impatient for my *petit pain au chocolate*—my favorite delicious chocolate-filled croissant —at Les Tuileries on our way home. Then she sang for Mr. Goldberg, not a Hans Christian Anderson song, nor my bedtime song, but one that sounded like my mother's records.

"Why were you singing for him?" I asked as we were leaving.

"He wanted to hear my voice so he could give me some ideas about who would be a good teacher for me."

"Is that why you came to live with us?"

"Yes, partly, but also because I got tired of living in New Jersey, where so many people didn't like me because my skin is brown, so I decided to come to Europe to become a singer."

As a child, I thought a lot about what it would be like to have someone not like me because my skin was a different color. I had already lived many places where my skin was a different color, but no one had hated me for it. She told me it was called racism, and the darker your skin, the more people would judge you.

This was the beginning of my lifelong exploration of otherness, and when people feel "othered," and by whom, and what responsibility did I have as a person of privilege and entitled whiteness to undo that injustice. *"Big shoes to fill . . ."* for a little girl.

∾   ∾   ∾

The spring of my fourteenth year, two brothers, with skin as dark as my father's favorite ebony carvings, were staying with us, visiting from Liberia. One was a year older than me, one a year younger. It was not uncommon for us to have houseguests from anywhere in the world. We decided to go to a movie, where I saw some friends from school. *"Je t'ai vu au ciné avec deux garçons noirs, très noirs . . ."*[12] I could hear their unspoken question: Who were these *black* boys, and what was I doing with them?

Earlier that week, in the whispered gossip of high school girls, I heard the rumor that a married woman had given birth to a brown baby—juicy gossip for this community of Calvinists, who hid behind the cloak of sameness and whiteness. Who was the father? They all wanted to know, because her husband was white. I was startled to realize this was a big deal, for my life had always included welcoming differences of skin tone.

ॐ   ॐ   ॐ

Although my family, living in the global environment we were in, always welcomed people of different races from all over the world, it took many years for me to realize my family's graciousness did not always extend to people of different class backgrounds.

---

12. Translation: "I saw you at the movies with two black boys, very dark . . ."

One year, midway through my career as a classroom teacher, I took a leave of absence to teach at The Evergreen State College as visiting faculty in a coordinated studies program called Third World Focus on Early Childhood Development. In some of the best teaching of my career, my teaching partner and I integrated what we now call Cultural Competence with Child Development, as we developed culturally relevant and developmentally appropriate curriculum. My teaching partner was a Lakota woman who coordinated Indian education for the Olympia School District. One night a week I stayed with my grandmother in her assisted-living facility. She had lived and traveled all over the world, often entertaining or being entertained by royalty. I explained that my co-teacher was Indian.

"Does she wear a sari?" my grandmother wanted to know.

"I beg your pardon?" I was confused.

"Ahh," it suddenly dawned on me that the only *Indian* in the realm of her experience came from India. When I explained I meant *Indian*, as in *indigenous American*, she frowned, pursed her lips and was silent. I could see her judging eyes, with visions of panhandling drunks in Seattle's Pioneer Square. Her judgment was an iceberg tip in my family's inability to truly embrace differences across lines of class and education. I know these tapes from previous generations still live on in me.

My first husband, now deceased, once haughtily mimicked me: "I have a master's degree from Bank Street College of

Education . . ." Did I really sound that pompous? Evidently, in his perception I did. In his eyes, it was fine for me to simply be a "school teacher," but when I took a job as a "professor" at an institution of higher learning, it was more than he cared to handle.

₮   ₮   ₮

These questions—raised by my childhood experiences— questions of safety, of identity, of belonging, of self-confidence and worth are not just personal ones. They are universal human questions. Each of us has faced them: Who is there for me? Will I be safe? Where do I belong? Who believes in me? Am I good enough? How do I treat others?

The foundational threads of my family's values woven together with my life experiences make me who I am. These threads have held strong, as both guide and anchor. How have I woven them into my own life as a teacher? If I live from a place of wholeness and integrity, *who I am* will permeate all that I do as a teacher. My capacity to understand my students is directly related to my capacity to understand myself. By remembering my own experience of the impact of my own struggles with those universal human questions, I can better understand how my students experience their own lives.

"We teach who we are."
—Parker Palmer

Chapter Two

On Children

Children . . . need most of the same things adults need— consideration, respect for their work, the knowledge that they and the things they do are taken seriously.[13]

After being in the classroom for fifteen years, I moved into teacher education. As the director of a graduate teacher certification program in a small college in the Pacific Northwest, I used to tell my graduate students that their ability to connect with their students depended on the degree to which they knew and trusted their own selfhood. I tried a shorthand visual way of getting that message across:

---

13. Caroline Pratt, *I Learn from Children* (New York, NY: Cornerstone Library, 1971), 43.

Believe what you see

Know what you believe

I stuck those words in adhesive black cutout letters on a magnifying shaving mirror, and hung it on the bulletin board. The subtle circular message multiplied:

- Look at yourself—closely—your magnified and magnificent reflection.
- When you look at yourself, trust what you see and know who you are, believe in yourself.
- Come to know what you believe—about yourself, about your students, and about teaching and learning.
- When you look at children, trust what you see, know who they are and believe in them.

Believe what you see . . . know what you believe . . . This means remembering how our own childhood answers those "universal questions" of belonging and safety. It means remembering how our own stories affect our approach to life. It means bringing forward our understanding from these experiences as we engage children in becoming all that they can be. Only then can we teach.

We need to pay attention not only to *who* is the self that teaches but also to *who* is the self that learns. Just as Parker Palmer has noted about teaching, we can also talk of what to *learn*, or *how to learn*, and even philosophically *why we learn*, but more importantly, *who* is the child that learns? And how does the quality of my relationship with that child form—or deform—his or her capacity to learn? What makes it possible for both teacher and learner to "show up" with all of who they are? Teaching and learning co-create each other: teacher and child in a complex dance of give and take, embracing both *I* and *Thou*, and together building avenues for peace where everyone has a place, where everyone belongs.

Thinking back, which of my own teachers do I, as an adult, remember the best? The ones with whom I connected, the ones with whom I built a relationship—and much more meaningfully than the content of their lessons, the ones who believed in me. The teacher I remember the best was my ninth grade Latin teacher, Mme Bouvier, who saw me and allowed me to see her. A mother of five, married to a paraplegic man who died that year, she still had room to love us all, and inspired our humanity, our compassion, and our creativity. How can a Latin teacher inspire creativity? She challenged us as a group to build a model of a Roman camp, and take it "on tour" throughout the school, charging ten *centimes* admission to raise money for a class field trip.

As a teacher, if I put distance between myself and my students, I have missed an opportunity for relationship, for connection, whether my students are adults or young children. With any age learner, I try to model my thinking, my questioning, my joys as well as my concerns. Teaching is first about building relationships. The teachers I loved were the ones with whom I had a relationship, the ones who *saw* me. As a teacher, I relearned this lesson early on in my career.

When my youngest son, Luke, came home from his first day of middle school (and his first experience with a rotation of teachers), he declared, "Well, I have only one teacher who is a real person . . ." He has always had good antennae for *realness*.

If a child is going to learn, she or he must feel safe and seen, encouraged to bring all of who they are. If we don't want children to leave themselves at the door of the classroom, we must also enter with all of who we are. Florida Scott Maxwell says, "You need only claim the events of your life to make yourself yours. When you truly possess all you have been and done . . . you are fierce with reality."[14] Young children are always "fierce with reality," and they quickly sense whether we are real.[15] To meet them where they are, we must also be fierce with reality.

---

14. Florida Scott Maxwell, *The Measure of My Days* (New York: Penguin Books, 1983), 42.

15. Parker Palmer, *The Courage to Teach,* 7.

As I told my graduate students many times, I learn from children, and if I am no longer learning from children, I have no business being their teacher. At a school assembly honoring my retirement, I spoke of the many lessons I had learned from the children gathered before me: lessons of joy and loving life, of caring and compassion, of curiosity and wonder, of patience and perseverance, of responsibility and respect, and lessons of fairness and forgiveness. These are not lessons of math and reading and writing one might typically expect at an elementary school, but the lessons of life; and the children were my teachers. Even as I taught teachers, my heart never left the children. Their wisdom, wit, insight, and compassion continue to give me hope and courage: courage to live and love with integrity, and hope that we might as a nation, as a world, come together to tap the power of *us* through our children. As Gandhi reminds us, "If we are to reach real peace in the world, we shall have to begin with the children."

ॐ   ॐ   ॐ

I had a favorite T-shirt:[16]

... my head is full of children ...

I gave it to a Ugandan pineapple farmer whose head was also full of children. When he was twelve, his father died and he dropped out of school to become the head of his household. He vowed that his eight siblings and the children of his village would not go without an education, and built a school on his land.

---

16. Design by artist Kiki Suarez. Used by permission of the artist. The black-and-white reproduction doesn't do justice to the brilliant captivating colors.

Whenever I wore my T-shirt to school, invariably a child, captured by the brilliant colors and the magical image on my chest, would stop to read the words. Emily, a literal-minded beginning reader, looking up at my shirt, haltingly decoded:

"my. . . head. . . is. . . full. . . of. . . children. . ." Her eyes widened. She looked up at my head. "Really?" she asked, incredulous.

"Really," I said, "my heart too."

I would also like to design a T-shirt to read:

...my heart is full of children...

Is my heart big enough to hold them all?

Aishah, who came into my office saying she needed to pray —it was during Ramadan—and knelt down bowing her head to the floor, and who somehow at age six knew which way to turn toward Mecca. And Ricky, a bright but disturbed seven-year-old with diagnoses as long as your arm, who on Halloween bit a classmate on the neck; he was "sharpening his vampire teeth." And Deondre, whose mother had mutilated his genitals and then abandoned him, and whose grandmother, the only rock in his young life, had just died. And Wilson, who always went down on his knees in my presence, calling me Madam, a sign of respect he learned so well in his native Ghana. The school psychologist labeled him with ADHD (attention deficit hyperactivity disorder). I refused to give his mother the psychologist's paperwork, as I knew it was merely our inability to fully understand his cultural context. How did these children, and so many others, find their way into my heart? How could these children not have found their way into my heart once I knew their stories?

𐆎 𐆎 𐆎

I have only recently begun to think of my teaching as "peacemaking," though I have always been drawn to speak up for "children who are not yet peaceful,"[17]especially those who are challenged by violence, or racism, or poverty. Parker Palmer describes violence as "any way we have of violating the identity and integrity of another human being."

> *Violence is done when parents insult children, when teachers demean students, when supervisors treat employees as disposable means to economic ends, when physicians treat patients as objects, when people condemn gays and lesbians "in the name of God," when racists live by the belief that people of a different skin color are less than human. And just as physical violence may lead to bodily death, spiritual violence causes death in other guises—the death of a sense of self, of trust in others, of risk-taking on behalf of creativity, of commitment to the common good. If obituaries were written for deaths of this*

---

17. Title of a book by Donna Bryant Goertz (Berkeley, CA: North Atlantic Books, 2001)

kind, every daily newspaper would be a tome.[18]

Many children in schools, especially children of color or of poverty, experience daily micro-aggressions, daily violence against their sense of identity. Through subtle forms of dismissiveness—a look, a word, or a non-word—children can feel marginalized, made to feel "other," as if the world were not really meant for them.

> *When someone with the authority of a teacher, say, describes the world and you are not in it, there is a moment of psychic disequilibrium, as if you looked into a mirror and saw nothing.*[19]

As a teacher, I always want the mirror of my classroom to reflect the lives of my students, so that they may each feel seen and heard. So that when they look in that mirror, they come to believe that they belong, that they are cared for; that they can feel safe, respected, and competent. When I understand this, all my teaching becomes about peacemaking, about "peace and justice for all." What do I do to reflect the lives of the children I teach? How do I hear their voices?

       ॐ   ॐ   ॐ

---

18. Parker J. Palmer, *A Hidden Wholeness: The Journey Toward an Undivided Life* (San Francisco, CA: Jossey-Bass, 2004), 169.

19. Adrienne Rich, *Blood, Bread and Poetry,* chapter 13 (1986). From an essay written in 1984.

When I was ten years old in Geneva, my favorite time of the week was babysitting the two-year-old son of family friends. I was paid ten *centimes* an hour, though I would have gladly paid for the privilege. We could be seen riding together: me on my bike, with him on the handlebars. I could just barely see over his head, and it made steering a bit challenging. One day I had to brake quite suddenly, and he toppled forward. Fortunately, I was wearing a skirt and his heels caught under the hem of my skirt. He hung there upside down until I could pull him upright. When our parents found out, they immediately put a stop to our riding double.

I loved how his language was exploding every day. I remember one day a full moon was visible in the daytime.

"Moon," he said.

"Yes, moon," I echoed.

"My moon," he declared.

My own young mind tried to understand his thinking. Could we each have our own moon? "My moon, too," I replied. I tried to get inside his head as he struggled with the possibility of sharing one moon.

"Sharing one moon" means being willing to experience another perspective. As an adult I still wonder: If we can share one moon, can we also share one earth, one world? Can we envision a world beyond the boundaries that separate us: nation, race, class, and creed? Can we embrace a world where we truly become *us*?

Wondering about "sharing one moon" so many years ago, was when I began to "listen beyond words." My father used to despair because, other than the comics, the only part of the newspaper I ever read growing up was Art Linkletter's column on "Kids Say the Darndest Things." Some of it was *cute*, or *amusing* as my father saw it, but some of it, in my mind, was quite profound. Even as a child I was fascinated.

Young children try to make sense of the world long before they have the words to express the connections they make. When my son, Luke, was two, we were at a lakeside cottage, visiting friends. They had a wood-burning hot tub. The adults were filling the hot tub with pail after pail of lake water; then they built a fire in the adjacent box to heat the water. Six months later, when Luke's language had developed enough for him to articulate his observation, he asked, "Why were Joe and Nancy putting water in their fireplace?" His experience with mixing water and fire was limited to the campfires we put out with water.

A few months later, Luke was outside with a rake, making a pile of leaves fallen from our large maple tree.

"I'm leaving," he informed me.

"Where are you going?" I asked.

"No, I'm leaving with a rake . . . ."

Luke was applying his budding understanding of the structure of language, and forming his own new verb.

ॐ   ॐ   ॐ

Language is one window into children's thinking. When I taught the Human Development course to my graduate students, I always gave a Child Study assignment. They were to observe and record what a young child said and did, as a way to begin to understand what goes on in a child's mind, how he or she makes sense of the world.

I told them I always try to listen to the words of children as a way into their thinking, into their understanding of the world. If half of language is listening, then my job as the listener is also to be available to reshape children's ever-expanding understanding of the world, as they take in new information, and as their capacity to understand different realities expands.

When my son Nik was four, we had listened together to a news report on farmers' concerns over the growing wolf population. He complained that wolves were breaking the "law of not killing." Most four-year-olds see the world in black-and-white with strict and predictable rules. I explained that animals don't have laws like people; that laws were made for and by people.

"Sure animals have laws," he declared, "haven't you ever

seen the signs on the road for deer, telling them where to cross so they don't get squished?"

A few months later, when his grandfather went off to speak to a church group, Nik asked what his grandfather's speech was going to be about.

"How people should get along in the world." I replied.

"Is Grandpa going to die?" I reassured him it would happen at some point, but not immediately. He was quiet for a while, and then asked, "No, I mean is Grandpa going to get killed?"

I tried to understand his thinking.

"Well," he said, "Martin Luther King said people should get along in the world, and he got killed; Jesus said people should get along in the world, and he got killed. Is Grandpa going to get killed?"

ക   ക   ക

While language is a window into a children's thinking, I shared with my graduate students that, as an educator and a parent, I felt my job was also to *listen beyond words*, beyond actions, to the belief behind the behavior, to the context behind the words, to the reality of a child's life. Unless I listen beyond what is immediately in front of me, I have no way of knowing what is below the surface. What I see and hear is just the tip of the iceberg.

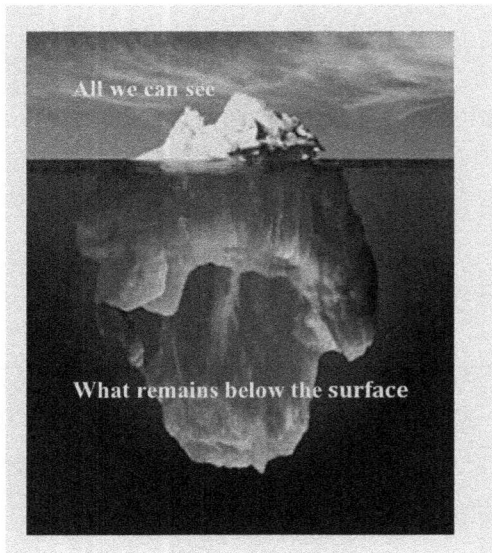

To find out what is beneath the surface, I need to start not with the *what* of their actions or words, but with the *who*—asking myself: "Who is this child?" "What makes this child come alive?" "How can I create a sense of safety for this child's spirit?" "How can I help this child develop a sense of competence, of curiosity, of compassion?" I need to listen beyond their words.

↾   ↾   ↾

Listening Beyond Words

There are words in me
    that keep leaking out
    around the edges,
words that have no sound,
    no voice,
and yet they speak out
    in the language
    before language—
a touch, a look, a smile,
a heart that flies open,
    winged by grace,
grace that leaks out
    around the edges.
I want to belong.
Seeking a home
    but have no welcome.[20]

Often, more than my words, it was a *touch*, a *smile*, an invitational *look* I brought to children that helped to unlock their sense of welcome and safety. So it was with Demarcus, a memorable child from my first year as a teacher in New York City.

---

20. Poem written on September 11, 2010, while I was participating in a retreat led by John Fox, poet and author of *Poetic Medicine.*

"Why does Demarcus always get snack first?" they wanted to know, this group of six-year-olds.

"Because he is afraid there won't be enough and he won't get any," I replied. How did I know this? By sensing the language beyond language. I watched Demarcus's agitation every time we had snack, his two-handed grab into the basket of graham crackers, and the relaxation of his body as the food reached his mouth. My job is to speak up, to give voice when it is a child's behavior that speaks. Even six-year-olds can understand worry and feel empathy; they simply wanted an explanation. They weren't upset or envious or feeling jealous. No one asked: What about me? I was teaching them about life in community, where each person understands and accepts that we each have different needs.

I will never forget Demarcus, his earnest face, his rich dark-brown, beautiful eyes, and, at times, impish grin. He was the second-born in his family, just eleven months after his older brother. He had a younger sister, and his mother, a single parent, was seven months pregnant.

The group was unusually noisy that day, and I turned off the lights to get their attention. Demarcus started screaming, "No, no," he shouted, as he darted around the room, his hands over his ears. "Don't ever turn off the lights!" That got the group's attention, even when I had struggled to do so. I turned the lights back on, and Demarcus calmed down. I found out that the power in his apartment had been turned off because his mother hadn't been able to pay the bill. I never again used turning off the lights as a signal for getting a group's attention.

Demarcus's outbursts were frequent, but usually short-lived. With physical proximity and touch he was able to calm down. One day when he was particularly out of sorts and having a meltdown, my assistant and I exchanged glances. She took him into the room across the hall, where we sometimes worked one-on-one with a child. She held him on her lap, and the tension gradually released from his body. She started to tell him a story, knowing that anything to capture his attention would help dispel whatever demons were tormenting him. The story featured a little dog that was lost and trying to find someone to take care of him. Demarcus stopped her. "Was the dog brown or white?", he wanted to know, his earnest brown eyes longing to find his place in the world. Over the year he slowly began to trust, began to make sense of the world and his place in it. He learned to read that year.

In listening to children, I certainly learn from them. How do I hear their voices? They inspire me to move beyond myself to ask bigger questions, the questions of hope—hope for learning, hope for understanding. They inspire me to continue learning. They teach me to delight in their realness, in their curiosity, in their openhearted view of the world. More than their language, it is their pre-language that fascinates me, the words that leak out around the edges, soundless yet full of meaning. We have much to learn from children, if we are paying attention.

As a result of growing up the way I did, I developed the skills of observation—it was a matter of survival. Because I often didn't speak the language, I developed the ability to listen beyond words. I also developed compassion, the ability to empathize, to feel what others are feeling. My own family values and childhood experiences have helped me to extend my heart to those whose voices have been silenced, to those who find themselves invisible or marginalized.

These children, and many others, have found their way into my heart. Is my heart big enough to hold them all? My career as an educator centers on speaking up for children who may not have had the privilege of having a loving parent, a warm place to sleep, and adequate sustenance. More than merely speaking up *for* them, I have encouraged them to find their own voice, their place in the world. Just as I, as a child, explored some of those universal human questions of life, about meaning and belonging—as we each do—my role as a teacher is to help children do the same.

- *Where do I belong? Will I be safe?*
- *Who is there for me? Who believes in me?*
- *Where is my place in the world? Am I good enough?*
- *How do I treat others?*

෨   ෨   ෨

Where do I belong? Will I be safe?

Kurt was a wiry six-year-old with a scruff of blond hair. His eyes darted about the room, as if seeking some invisible enemy. For the third time that week, his teacher, Martha, called me in to remove him from his first-grade classroom, where he was disrupting his classmates' learning. Ignoring his behaviors had only resulted in escalation.

Though sullen when he saw me, he seemed relieved to have someone take charge of his behavior and his lack of self-control. Knowing he had "flipped his lid"[21] and was not in an emotional state to be very rational about understanding his behavior, I simply asked him to help me with a basket of markers to check which ones needed to be thrown out because they were dead. This was a tactic I used with many children who needed to reconnect with a place of being able to calm themselves. I confess to rescuing from the trash can markers that had been deemed dead, just for this purpose.

He sat at a table in my office, his face releasing a bit of its scowl, and his shoulders relaxing a bit. I went about answering e-mails at my desk. After a few minutes, I asked if he would be willing to help me with an important job, removing the staples from a large bulletin board in the hall; that job required a special tool and I thought he would be good at it.

---

21. A term coined by Daniel Siegel, MD, used to describe actions that come from the reptilian brain, rather than the more rational prefrontal cortex part of the brain.

I wanted to get him out of my office, where other children walking by might look in and think, "Oooh—Kurt is in trouble again . . ."

As we started picking the staples out of the wall, I asked him for his ideas about where he thought we should collect them. He promptly got a chair to collect the fruits of our labor. Already he seemed to feel a little more important, a little more like he belonged. After a few minutes, I commented, "Having a bad day, aren't you?" hoping I hadn't moved too quickly, and that he was sufficiently in control to not get defensive.

"Yeah," he said, and then pausing, he blurted, "I'm mad because I don't have any friends."

I resisted the urge to lecture: "Well, of course you don't have any friends, look at how you are treating people . . ." Instead I asked him what he would like to do about it.

"I don't know what to do," his voice echoing the defeat in his body.

"Would you like to put it on the Class Meeting agenda?"[22]

"Yeah."

I knew there was sometimes a backlog of agenda items and that he might have to wait several weeks before being able

---

22. Classrooms in our school held daily Class Meetings, where children took charge of respectfully solving problems.

to talk about this. "Shall we go put it on the agenda right now?"

"OK."

"Kurt has something for the class meeting agenda," I announced to the whole class upon our reentry, and privately to his teacher, "It needs to be now."

This class usually concluded their day with their class meeting, and it was near the end of the day, so I stayed.

"I have a problem I need help with," I heard Kurt say, his voice strong and confident. "I have a problem. I don't have any friends and that makes me sad and angry and makes me act bad."

If there had been an empathy switch, he had triggered it, and soon had all kinds of offers, framed in self-advocating. "I like you, and I want to play with you, but I don't like it when you are mean, so you can play with me, but you have to agree not to be mean, can you agree?" I had tears in my eyes, knowing what a powerful moment this was, not only for Kurt but also for the classroom climate and culture. The children later dubbed "Class Meeting" as the "magic circle," for it seemed that insurmountable problems were magically resolved.

           ❧   ❧   ❧

What I learned from children on that day was to trust them to know what they need. To trust they know how to show empathy, and mostly to listen on a deeper level, to the hurt and pain behind the behavior. As Parker Palmer says, "Violence is what we do when we don't know what else to do with our pain and suffering."[23] What can we all learn from children, who still have the capacity to believe in the goodness of the human heart?

In speaking up for Kurt, my goal was to create a safe space that empowered him to advocate for himself and to develop a sense of competence, and thereby a sense of belonging. Feeling competent and confident can only develop once you know you have been seen. Truly seeing children is a way to *speak up for a child.* This is how I try to teach.

ॐ   ॐ   ॐ

More than once I encountered other children who managed to find it in themselves to be there for another child.

"Keep them away from me!" Bo screamed, eyes wild with fear, frantic. He alternately hid, then ran in circles, slashing the air as if fencing off shadows only he could see. I had observed similar behavior in his older cousin, with whom he lived. All I could think of was Pol Pot's violence, but Bo was a Cambodian child born in the United States well after the horrors of war his parents had witnessed. Is it possible to

---

23. Parker J. Palmer, *Healing the Heart of Democracy: The Courage to Create a Politics Worthy of the Human Spirit* (San Francisco, CA: Jossey-Bass, 2011), 19.

inherit PTSD (Post Traumatic Stress Disorder)? Genetically or environmentally? My conclusion in this instance, and from my own experience of witnessing violence early in my life, was yes. When he was again calm, I asked if there was anyone who could help in times when he felt so desperate. "Yes," he said, "Josh can stay with me."

We went to ask him. Josh, only eight years old, had a depth of wisdom beyond his years. He had watched this outburst, and rather than being fearful, he was filled with compassion. "Yes," he said, "I can do that. I will stay with you until you calm down."

The innate wisdom of children goes beyond anything I could possibly teach them. The best way to invite a child's whole being to show up is to be authentically all of who we are, including our pain and our shadows.

ॐ   ॐ   ॐ

Who is there for me? Who believes in me?

One of the ways I continue to advocate for children is in my role as a CASA (Court Appointed Special Advocate) for children in foster care, sometimes also known as a *guardian ad litem*. One of my visits to a child in my caseload took me to a middle school. I went to sign the visitors' book, expecting the secretary to wave with a cursory "you know where to find him," as I had been there many times before. Instead, I noticed her brief hesitation and an exchange of glances between the office staff. "Just a minute," she said, "this may not be a good day." The assistant principal then appeared and beckoned me to follow her.

As we walked through the maze of halls typical of so many large, urban secondary schools, she informed me that Jason had had a problem that morning and was now in detention.

"What set him off?" I inquired.

"He didn't want to do his math work, but preferred to read a book. He and the aide really got into it, and he became violent—a battle of wills."

When I arrived where he was being detained, there were three adults, two of whom were holding the door handle shut. I read their body language as fear. I could hear cussing and crashing from within the room. The "room," one used to contain kids with out-of-control behavior, was empty of all furniture, nothing short of a padded cell, except that Jason had put his fist through the wallboard and was in the process of systematically trashing the room by ripping the wallboard off the walls.

"Let go of the handle," I told the office staff. Startled, they backed off. The sound from inside the room stopped. "Hey, Jason," I called through the door, "I brought you a book, but it looks like you're having a bad day . . ."

Silence.

"Just leave it outside the door," his voice now steadying.

"No," I replied, "I'll bring it back on a better day; I want to give it to you in person."

Silence. I opened the door.

"Hey, man, it's good to see you . . ."

I hadn't realized I had been holding my breath. Even though I knew he wouldn't hurt me, my relief was evident.

Jason was sitting on the floor, with his back against the wall, his elbows propped on his knees, his head in his hands. He looked up, relieved to see a friendly face.

"I'm not going to let them win . . ." he muttered beneath his breath. His jaw was tight, but his eyes held mine.

"You know this isn't about winning or losing, Jason, it's about getting along."

He nodded. "I just want to be treated like a human being," I could hear him say in his mind, words he could not say to his abusive stepfather.

Now calm, he stood and walked over to me. The assistant principal, the counselor, and the aide stood back, simply watching the transformation.

"Do you think you are ready to go back to class and try again, and let's look at that math that is giving you a hard time?" I handed him the book I had brought.

"Thanks," was all he said.

So often it is the system that forgets to treat each child with the same respect you would want for yourself. Children's behavior should be listened to, children should be seen, and heard, and believed.

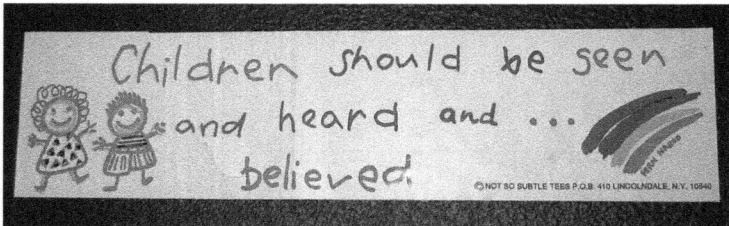

Children should be seen and heard and ... believed.

Another setting where I worked, and where out-of-control behavior was frequently manifested, was a residential treatment school for adolescent boys. Many of the boys were wards of the state, abandoned by or removed from a parent's care. Robbie was seventeen. He was brought to the school at age eleven, after killing both of his parents with a shotgun while they slept. He had no memory of the incident, in the iceberg beneath his conscious memory. In the visible part of his iceberg, he could barely read. Every day he would come to our house for tutoring and loved to play with my son Nik, then only a few months old. While I felt confident he wouldn't harm Nik, I never left them alone. Robbie had some basic decoding skills, but lacked practice in reading and had no sense of making meaning from print. I gave him the novel *Papillon* to read, a thick book with small print, many pages and no pictures—quite a challenge. I told him the story was about a man held captive on an island and his attempts to escape.

He was intrigued with the story line, which mirrored his own sense of being "held" against his will at a school that happened to be on an island. It took him three months to read. No book reports due. I required nothing more of him, though I expected he would be so drawn in by the story that he would engage. No learning can happen without engagement, not just of the mind, but also of the soul. He handed me the book back, saying, "I finished it. Can I read it again?"

"Of course . . ." I hoped my smile wouldn't betray my deeper internal elation, for I didn't want him reading to please me.

Another way to speak up for children is to get out of their way. My intention is always to open doors as an invitation, to draw them in, to pique their curiosity, not to lead or push, or even point the way, unless they ask.

☙   ☙   ☙

Where is my place in the world?
Am I good enough?

The world into which you were born
is just one model of reality.
Other cultures are not
failed attempts at being you;
they are unique manifestations
of the human spirit.[24]

The intercom in my office rang. Marco's teacher called for me—again. He was uncooperative and unwilling to stay in his seat, wandering around the room, and disrupting her lesson on the Civil Rights Movement. When I arrived in his class, the other twenty-eight fifth-graders were in their seats, taking turns reading aloud about Selma and Montgomery and the bus boycott. The teacher occasionally stopped the reading to ask a comprehension question. The homework assignment was on the board: read chapter six from the textbook and summarize it.

I walked over to Marco; he greeted me a little warily, not quite knowing if I was there to reprimand him or rescue him. "What are you guys reading about?" I asked.

---

24. Wade Davis, from a poster published by the Syracuse Cultural Workers. 2003.

"I don't know; it's boring," a ten-year-old's ubiquitous judgment of anything they fear or don't understand. I invited him out into the hall.

"How old is your grandma?" I asked.

"You can't ask that; it's not polite." I knew his beloved grandmother was the only stable force in his life.

"About . . ." I backed off from my perceived impertinence.

"About sixty . . ."

"Where did she grow up?"

"Mississippi . . ." He pronounced it "Miss-ssippi." "Why?"

"Marco, I am giving you some homework, and you don't have to do the assignment on the board. I want you to go home and interview your grandmother. Ask her what it was like to grow up in Mississippi. Ask her what she was doing in 1955, in 1960, in 1965. Ask her if she ever met Martin Luther King Jr. or Rosa Parks. That's your homework, to write her story."

He was excited, but had so little experience of meaningful schoolwork that he threw up his own roadblocks.

"But . . . my teacher . . . she won't let me . . ."

"I will tell her I said it is okay."

The teacher accepted my alternative assignment for Marco,

though wanted to make sure I wasn't intending to craft personalized assignments for each student. Marco returned to class and sat down to listen in a new way. Rarely have I ever intervened in a teacher's lesson without being asked, but in this case, with a child who felt so invisible, so marginalized by the educational system, I knew I had to speak up. Looking into the mirror of his textbook, Marco could not see himself. As Adrienne Rich reminds us, "When someone with the authority of a teacher, say, describes the world and you are not in it, there is a moment of psychic disequilibrium, as if you looked into a mirror and saw nothing."

It doesn't take much to provide mirrors that can and do reflect the lives of our children. So many times, in so many schools, our lessons, our curriculum materials don't reflect the lives of the children we teach. Can we take the time to bring relevant material to our children?

For a number of years I taught a class called Emergent Curriculum to my graduate students. My basic message was "Start with the children, build from there, build on their knowledge and skills, on their interests." We sometimes now call that instructional philosophy "differentiated instruction." Curriculum material is relevant when a child sees her or himself reflected.

∾   ∾   ∾

Y our books are ready," the director of children's literature from Third Place Books called over to me. She had set aside a thirty-inch stack of brand new picture books, about fifty different titles—a donation to the Early Learning Center in rural Uganda that I was helping to build.

Excited, I sat in my car as I perused this windfall, scanning the titles. With each book, my enthusiasm fell a notch. I couldn't take these books: *Halloween Tricks and Treats, Thanksgiving in New England, My First Snow.* I realized that a children's book that might delight a North American child could be totally irrelevant to the life of a rural African child. I realized less than a quarter of the books were appropriate to take with me, mostly alphabet and counting books.

I thought back to the experience I had during my first trip to Uganda, when I was asked if I wanted to see the school's library and was taken to a metal cabinet with a sprung latch. A jumble of books and magazines lay on the shelf: the Yellow Pages from a small Midwestern town, a Sears catalog from 1976, a tattered textbook on the history of the American Revolution, all obsolete and irrelevant, donated by those who would pass discards off to *poor African children.* My heart sank. Help is not always helpful. These castoffs constituting the school's library broke my heart and left me outraged. I was not going to repeat such an act of disrespect.

I went to talk to Molly at my local bookstore about my dilemma. She and I spent the better part of an hour looking for books that would be more relevant. We traded my lovely —but culturally inappropriate books—for titles I felt comfortable taking with me. And while the trade wasn't one for one, at least I came away with a careful selection of books in which African children could hopefully see themselves represented. It doesn't take much to think about cultural relevance, and yet it takes a lifetime of learning to actually speak up and act. I am still learning.

છે   છે   છે

A year later, as I sat under a mango tree reading an alphabet book to a group of eager five- and six-year-old Ugandan children, I was again struck by the irrelevance of the pictures to their active lives. Their own environment abounded with rich learning materials, waiting to be tapped. I decided right then to create an alphabet book with photographs of familiar local objects, and spent the next two weeks snapping pictures from A to Z, all with the children's help. "Madam Jeenee, what about TOES, what about NOSE, what about HOE, what about BASKET, what about BEANS?" And the result was an alphabet book with local images. What lessons could a child, anywhere in the world, learn from such a book?

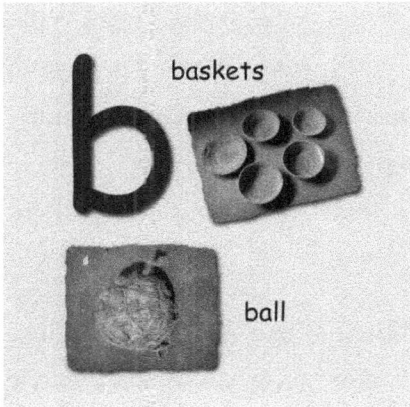

The "ball" is made from an inflated plastic bag wrapped with banana fibers.

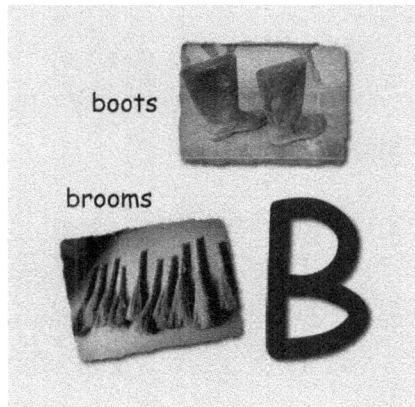

The "brooms" are made from a local weed.

On my next visit I brought fifty copies of this alphabet book to these very same young children in the Ugandan village.[25] Tears welled up in my eyes as I watched them—most had never held a book before. They eagerly poured over images familiar to them, exclaiming excitedly to one another as

---

25. The *Kyababeezi Alphabet Book* created by Jeanne Strong and the children of JEBMIDH Infant School and Kukanga Primary School. Available on Amazon.com.

they discovered in print what they saw in their own daily lives. I also used these books with two different groups of teachers as part of their learning about developmentally appropriate curriculum, and how to ask questions that help children deepen and expand their understanding of their world.

I was startled with the realization that two girls, whose photos appear on the *G* pages (for girls), did not recognize themselves until their classmates named them, for they had never seen their own image before—not even in a mirror! Every day I found my Western privileged assumptions challenged.

Years earlier, in my first year of teaching, I received a grant from the Polaroid Corporation—unlimited film and ten cameras. The first words the children learned to read were "YES" and "NO," the indication of whether there was enough light for a photo. The grant was to help these inner-city children see their world through the lens of a camera, and begin to learn to read by taking pictures of their surrounding world and creating their own alphabet book. When I created the *Kyababeezi Alphabet Book* I had forgotten those earliest alphabet books, using images familiar to children. There is indeed *a thread you follow . . .*

જ્જ   જ્જ   જ્જ

How do I treat others?

Awareness of differences can be taught. However, the social and cultural forces in the United States, especially in the media, can undermine those lessons. When my son Nik was four, we were in the grocery store buying some pancake syrup. He saw the Aunt Jemima pancake syrup, a brown bottle in the shape of a rotund woman, the quintessential stereotype of a mammy of plantation-slave days, complete with kerchief and apron.

"Let's get that one," he exclaimed, as he picked the bottle off the shelf.

"No, we're going to put that one back—I don't like it because it's a racist image."

"How do you know, Mom?" he replied, "It might be Harriet Tubman . . ."

Only two years later, he too had succumbed to the party line of societal role assumptions. After a visit to our family pediatrician, he came home and declared, "Dr. Wilson is really a nurse, we just call her 'doctor.'" Granted, he was developmentally at an age where making sense of the world by categorizing is a primary focus, and logic is based on preconceived ideas that are evolving and unfolding. At this stage you were either *this* or *that,* with little room for the ambiguity of *both—and*. In his mind she couldn't be both a doctor and a woman. Nonetheless, society's messages came through loud and clear.

Children at a young age notice differences, though initially do not attach value to them. These are differences they simply observe. Only through witnessing our own reactions, verbal or not, do they begin to make distinctions between *us* and *them*, and attach values. What responsibilities do we have as educators to help children continue to question the source of bias? We teach who we are, and our very body language communicates our values. There is no "value-free education," and we must constantly ask ourselves where and how our perceptions were formed.

ॐ   ॐ   ॐ

Early in my career as a classroom teacher I had an opportunity to question the perpetuation of bias. It was a Thursday afternoon, and school was just over for the day. Two girls in my school, both five years old—Chrissie, blue-eyed with long blonde curls and pale skin, and Emi, with shiny black hair and brown skin, adopted from South India by a white family—patiently waited for their mothers, who were chatting after school. I overheard Emi and Chrissie's conversation.

"What's the matter with you?" Chrissie said, "Did you fall in a mud puddle or something? Why are you so brown?"

I was shocked by her question, but I didn't have the courage or the words to speak up for this child who was being marginalized. My excuse was that it was after school, and the parents were standing right there, so it was their responsibility. I went home that night berating my silence.

A few weeks later, several children were in the art room working on a project, Emi and Chrissie among them. "Pass me the flesh tone crayon," said Maggie. I could not pass that one up, especially since in my own mind I was trying to redeem myself from my earlier silence.

"Whose flesh, Maggie?" I asked. "How can you say flesh tone? Is that the color of Emi's skin? Is it even the color of your skin?" I was unrelenting in my questioning. Maggie was a little startled by my uncharacteristic vehemence.

We abandoned the original art project, and I brought out my set of "people crayons" in all the shades of the human race, and the art lesson was transformed into finding the "people crayon" that most closely matched their own skin tone. Jackie, usually very quiet, suddenly asked, "What about flesh-colored Band-Aids, they probably don't match Emi's skin either; I know they don't match mine."

"Yeah . . ." Nods all around, from this group of mostly girls who were suddenly looking at one another in a new light.

The next day, in our morning class meeting we continued our discussion, and decided as a group to write a letter to the Johnson & Johnson Corporation, expressing our objection to the Band-Aids labeled as flesh colored, and to the Crayola Company on their labeling of crayons—probably the first social action from this group of elementary-school-age children.

Emi remained my student for several years, as the school was a multiage, ungraded elementary school, with continuous progress for each student. A few years later, during our morning meeting, Jeff was sharing that his grandfather had died and would be buried back in Kansas where he was born. Emi became visibly upset. I leaned over and touched her arm.

"What is it, Emi?"

"Do you always have to be buried where you were born?"

She was panicked at the thought of returning to an unknown and foreign land to be buried. I reassured her that that was Jeff's grandfather's choice, and there was no rule about where you had to be buried. She relaxed. Emi had built an elaborate fantasy about her origins, imagining that she was a princess who had lived in a castle, and yet the prospect of reality and fantasy colliding was more than she could bear.

It takes a sense of peace, a sense of well-being on the inside to be able to feel peaceful toward others. These are children whose young lives are fraught with uncertainty, with unpredictability. These children often feel invisible, often feel they don't belong, never quite felt sure who is there for them, uncertain of their own worth and competence; children who have been systematically made to feel "other."

A sense of competence can develop only once you know you have been seen, when you can recognize your uniqueness while being apart of something greater.

ॐ   ॐ   ॐ

Learning to not only accept but also welcome differences, and truly see each "other" creates a foundation for peace. Julie, the six-year-old who startled our classroom visitors by reminding us "we all read different books because we are all different people," on some level knew that school should be about learning to:

> *...discover how we fit together.*
> *My piece of the puzzle is not like anyone else's.*
> *My face holds the history of my people*
> *and the feelings of my heart.* [26]

Twenty-five years later, and some three thousand miles from where we first met, and quite serendipitously, Julie became my graduate student. She wanted to be a teacher.

If we could truly work to teach this—*to discover how we fit together*, to honor the uniqueness of each individual, their history and their feelings—perhaps the world would know greater peace, and we could live in a world where we can become *us*. As Holly Near says in her song "The Great Peace

---

26. Southern Poverty Law Center. *Teaching Tolerance,* no. 4 (Fall 1993).

March": "It is not an empty dream . . ." And *we must begin with the children.*

Chapter Three

Lessons from Children

I will never stop loving children; I love life too much.
—Paulo Freire[27]

When I first started teaching, I could not have articulated what I gradually came to believe about teaching and learning. I only knew I loved watching kids make sense of the world. I knew from my own childhood experiences that I wanted to belong, to be seen, to find my place in the world, to be connected to others. I knew I wanted the same for children. I knew I had a gift for listening beyond words, but I had little idea of what I believed or of all I would learn from children.

The pianist Michael Jones once said, "We have two glorious tasks: to be a good steward of the gift we are given and to wait upon that gift." I now understand that teaching and learning are gifts I both receive from and give to my students.

---

27. From a September 28, 1983, letter to schoolchildren in Gustavo Teixeira School in São Pedro, Brazil.

It is a symbiotic relationship. The gift I have been given is uniquely and innately my own and shaped by what has come before me, from generations past, as well as by my own life experiences. I have been a good steward of my gift, knowing that it could only be actuated by waiting and welcoming the gifts I receive from children. Without that, *my* gift is for naught.

The psychotherapist Virginia Satir, in the opening of her book *Making Contact,*[28] writes that the "greatest gift I can give is to see, hear, understand, and to touch another person. When this is done, I feel contact has been made." I have always thought of my teaching as making contact, guided in the way that Myles Horton, in a conversation with Paulo Freire, described leadership. He paraphrases Lao Tzu:

> *Go to the people. Learn from them. Live with them. Love them. Start with what they know. Build with what they have. But the best of leaders, when the job is done, when the task is accomplished, the people will all say we have done it ourselves.*[29]

My career as an educator has always been about something more than simply teaching. It has been about making a difference in one child's life, about making a difference in the life of a community. It is not by accident that midway

28. Virginia Satir, *Making Contact* (Berkeley, CA: Celestial Arts, 1995), 2.

29. Myles Horton and Paulo Freire, *We Make the Road by Walking*: *Conversations on Education and Social Change* (Philadelphia, PA: Temple University Press, 1990), 248.

through my career I found myself drawn into two different professional organizations that helped me expand my horizons as an educator. One, the Center for Courage and Renewal,[30] has a mission to reconnect who we are with what we do, "rejoining soul and role"[31] in personal and professional integrity. As a teacher, I experience the seamlessness between who I am and what I do. The other organization, the Positive Discipline Association,[32] is based on Adlerian psychology. Its mission is to develop respectful relationships in families, schools, and communities. I practiced creating respectful learning communities that honor the spirit of each child long before I ever knew that others had formed an organization based on what I had been doing for years. It is through my association with both the Center for Courage and Renewal and the Positive Discipline Association that I came to think of my teaching as "peacemaking" with children and adults alike, encouraging them to be all that they could be.

I once asked the director of teaching and learning for my school district if he would hire me as a "resident encourager," feeling that in this role I could support and encourage both students and teachers in a way that tapped many of my skills. With children or adults, how could I *not* create a learning community based on mutual respect, of self and others, honoring all of each individual, an approach that

---

30. Website: www.couragerenewal.org.

31. Parker J. Palmer, *A Hidden Wholeness: The Journey Toward an Undivided Life* (San Francisco, CA: Jossey-Bass, 2004), 13.

32. Website: www.positivediscipline.org.

invites connection and communication? Embracing the vision of a "resident encourager" brings together everything I believe about making the world a better place for all. The principles and practices of the Courage community deeply resonate with my beliefs about myself as a teacher: integrity and wholeness, authenticity and embracing diversity, creating community with courage, love, hope, and renewal. Given my family history, it was only natural for me to see my teaching as building peace and justice for all.

Over time, the many experiences I had with children became the foundational threads of my teaching, interwoven with the formative threads of my family's values and my own childhood experiences. These together shaped my approach to teaching and learning.

ॐ   ॐ   ॐ

The Shaping of Teaching and Learning

Elly, one of the many student teachers I mentored in my career, drove me crazy with her constant questions: "Why did you say that to that child? How did you decide to . . .? Why do you think . . .? What will you do?" At the end of her five-month stay in my classroom I thanked her—for her questions had forced me to explain why I did what I did, much of it done by intuition. Her questions also invited me to articulate and tease out the complexity of reasoning that goes into any interaction between teacher and student. They also helped me to see that while I treated children fairly, I did not necessarily treat them equally, for as young Julie reminded us, they "are all different people." It is now in retirement that I have the opportunity to more fully explore all that I have learned from children, the foundational building blocks that have shaped my teaching and learning.

My first teaching job was while a student at Oberlin College. The town of Oberlin was divided between the "college" and the "townies," racially and economically split, definitely divided by the ubiquitous railroad tracks. I was a French language major, an easy choice as I arrived fluent, and was taking a college course on Methods of Modern Language

Teaching. Most of my classmates were assigned students in the fourth grade gifted program, principally children of college faculty from the "right side" of the tracks, whose interest in learning a foreign language was deemed to be a worthy cause. For some reason I was given an after-school group, all girls as it turned out, who were from "the other side of the tracks." They had chosen to give up their free time to learn something called *French*. We met in a church basement.

Each Wednesday I prepared a lesson, trying to teach counting, basic greetings, and interesting vocabulary using objects, drawings, and flashcards. It was fall in this small Midwestern town, and horse chestnuts were plentiful. We counted chestnuts: "*Un marron, deux marrons, trois marrons, quatre marrons . . .*" I then pulled out some cartoon drawings of elephants, intending to also count them. I prompted them: "*Un . . .*" pointing to the *elephant*. (Did I choose that word because the spelling is identical in both French and English? Who knows what I was thinking?) They began: "*Un marron-elephant, deux marrons-elephants, trois marrons-elephants . . .*"

I learned one of my first big lessons in teaching:

1. *Check my assumptions.*

~œ   ~œ   ~œ

On our third weekly time together, the girls arrived in a bunch, glad to be there, and asked, "Can we just talk, before we do French?" So we talked; mostly I listened and possibly, eventually, we got to French. I learned then my second and third big lessons in teaching:

2. *Listen.*

3. *Build relationships.*

Listening and building relationships come before content. Without consciously knowing it, these three cornerstone lessons: (1) *check my assumptions,* (2) *listen,* and (3) *build relationships,* ingrained in me early in my career, etched into my very being, have served me well over a lifetime of teaching.

The next day, during one of our seminars, my professor was encouraging me to become a French teacher. With crystal clarity that came from some deeper source of knowing, I replied, "I don't want to teach French; I want to teach children." I didn't fully understand what I was saying or why, but have grown over the years to appreciate that tender wisdom.

෴   ෴   ෴

The seeds of the next lesson were planted early on in my own experience in La Petite École Nouvelle in Paris, where I attended second and third grade, and where I had had the shaky start with my name change. What I remember most from third grade was the experiential learning. We read a story about Jacques, a runaway ten-year-old *matelot*,[33] who had been taken on as deckhand on a barge that traveled the rivers of France. It never occurred to me to wonder where his parents were or why he had run away, but at age eight the sense of adventure and independence was developmentally paramount. We read of Jacques's travels, studied the history of the châteaux he passed by, learned how he fished, built a large-scale relief map of the rivers of France in the middle of the classroom, studied Roman and Gothic architectural forms of the cathedrals he passed, took weekly field trips to examine and sketch Ionic, Doric, and Corinthian columns, learned how keystones work in vaulted arches. It was the hands-on learning I have never forgotten. Without a doubt it shaped who I became as a teacher, as I replicated that integrated, experiential curriculum in my first years of actual employment as a teacher.

That first elementary school, in the heart of New York City, was designed to be representative of the population of the city: one-third black, one-third Puerto Rican, and one-third other. Partially funded by a grant from the Sloan-Kettering Foundation, half the students were on some kind of scholarship, and half of those received a full scholarship, which meant their families were on welfare. The rich mix of cultural perspectives also shaped my idea of how to run a

---

33. French word for *sailor.*

democratic classroom, based on active and real-life learning.

With my group of lively six-year-olds I built our yearlong core curriculum on the theme of *The World Around Us,* guiding the learning to include all the basic skills appropriate for that age. We read and wrote about the history of Manhattan. We built a four-foot-by-eight-foot relief model of the island of Manhattan. We included each child's building, complete with water towers for buildings over seven stories, figuring out the ratio of building height: one centimeter equaled one story. We constructed the buildings out of two-by-twos, measured and sawed to size in our classroom shop. We learned how to make water go uphill by using a glass gallon cider jug and a bicycle pump. We built a model of the block around the school out of cardboard boxes, wiring each for electricity. We learned about different kinds of circuits: parallel and series. We interviewed each of the shopkeepers in the block, and wrote protest letters to animal rights groups about the animal fur shop. We traveled by subway to landmarks in Manhattan, using "tripmaps" to check off each stop. We toured Manhattan Island by boat, and produced a film of all the bridges around Manhattan, complete with music and a narrated history of each bridge.

A truly integrated curriculum, I was indeed re-creating my own early learning experiences. These were days, rich with possibility, of the Open Classroom, based on implementing the best of John Dewey's model for progressive education, where "children will learn when they are ready." Erik

Erikson conducted research on "play" in our school. Some of the earliest footage for *Sesame Street* was filmed in my classroom. I could not imagine teaching in any other way. We were learning together by doing.

Above my desk I posted the oft-quoted Chinese proverb:
> *I hear and I forget.*
> *I see and I remember.*
> *I do and I understand.*

To my early lessons of (1) *check my assumptions,* (2) *listen,* and (3) *build relationships*, I added a fourth:

4. *Learning together by doing . . .*

☘ ☘ ☘

In my third year of teaching I had a student teacher (I have conveniently forgotten her name) who spent a whole semester with me. Along about December she asked, "Do you ever teach them anything?"

I was stunned by her question and quickly swallowed my surprise and asked her what she meant.

"Get up in front of them and tell them..."

My heart sank. She had missed the whole point of my teaching. "No," I replied, "I guess I never teach them anything."

"But just look at all they are learning..." I silently screamed.

Her limited and rigid experience only recognized a model of education where the teacher tells and the student passively listens. I was so saddened that I was unable to even begin to explain what I was doing. I thought it should be obvious. It was only a few years later, however, that Elly, my student teacher who constantly pestered me with questions, helped me to articulate my philosophy.

     ∾   ∾   ∾

Part of what happens in an active classroom where teacher and children work collaboratively is a deepening sense of community. Under a sketched image of a pyramid of humans of a range of skin tones I hung one of my favorite posters on the wall of my classroom:

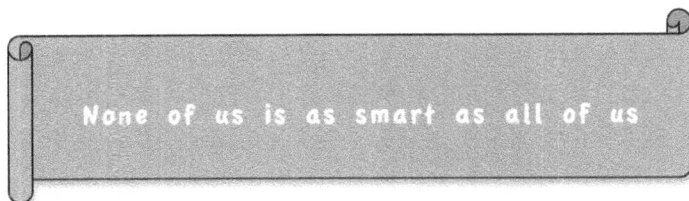

None of us is as smart as all of us

My classroom was indeed always designed to embrace shared learning, community building and cooperation. That poster reminds me of my son Luke, who at age five made the pronouncement: "No one person in the world knows everything, but all together we know everything." To my list of core lessons I added:

5. Build community.

I learned another powerful lesson in those years, from a statement made by an African American parent: "The open-classroom concept is a white middle-class luxury . . . My child, because of the color of his skin, needs to be on or above grade level if he is going to make it in the world . . ."

It has taken me many years to fully understand the implications of her statement—that it wasn't enough to have good intentions and interesting ideas if I didn't also give children the skills to compete in the world. Lisa Delpit, an African American professor, writes of *Skills and Other Dilemmas of a Black Progressive Educator,*[34] as she describes the need for teaching the tools of power to students who have been excluded, by race or poverty, from the privileges that come with white skin and money. I had the opportunity, years later, in graduate school to reexamine some of the shortcomings of Dewey's model of progressive education in a pluralistic society. Another opportunity for me to check my assumptions, with the added lesson:

6. Respect differences.

                  ☙   ☙   ☙

---

34. Lisa Delpit, *Other People's Children: Cultural Conflict in the Classroom* (New York, NY: The New Press, 1995), 11-20.

Building a Respectful Community

Over time, as I practiced these powerful lessons, they became habits, incorporated into my daily interactions. They anchored my teaching. By building on these cornerstones, I could create a respectful learning community. This was equally true in my classroom of children, in the adult community of my graduate students, and in the elementary school where, as a school administrator, I sought respectful solutions for teachers, parents, and students alike. My grounding from the organizations *Courage and Renewal* and *Positive Discipline* helped me to strengthen and shore up those anchors.

One year, in the elementary school where I was one of the administrative team, we had an inordinate amount of teasing and name-calling on the playground. I adapted an activity called "Charlie" from Positive Discipline, designed to teach mutual respect. I changed the name to "Bob," as we had a first-grader named Charlie, and no "Bobs" in the school. I asked two children to draw, on a large piece of butcher paper, a face of a near-expressionless child. In an all-school assembly of some 450 students, I told the story of Bob, how he was a boy who many kids didn't like, that he was new to the school, that he didn't have many friends, and other kids liked to tease him and make fun of him. I asked for some of the teasing words they might hear. Slowly the momentum picked up, they all knew the words that wound:

"You can't play."

"Get out of here."

"Why don't you go back to where you came from?"

"You're weird, stupid, ugly, dumb . . ."

With each put-down, I wrinkled "Bob's" face a little bit, until finally the whole butcher paper was wadded up and I threw it on the floor. You could have heard a pin drop.

I then asked for words that might make Bob feel better, words that heal:

"Will you be my friend?"

"Come play."

"You're good at kickball!" and with each affirmation, I unwrinkled Bob a bit, until the butcher paper was as flat as could be.

"What do you notice?" I asked. Several hands went up.

"He's still wrinkled . . ."

"Yes, hurtful, wounding words always leave wrinkles . . . even on real people."

Later in the day, following the assembly, a young kindergartner stopped me to ask: "Where is Bob now?" and in the weeks that followed, on more than one occasion, I witnessed children stopping themselves mid-sentence to change their wounding words.

ã»   ã»   ã»

We were three months into the school year and room 206 was still chaotic. Backbiting, defiance, disruptions, put-downs, and disrespect permeated the atmosphere in this third-grade classroom. Children did not feel safe; there was no *gemeinschaftsgefühl*, to use Alfred Adler's term for describing a sense of belonging and community interdependence. The manifestations of their dis-ease came out in their behavior. The full range of typical "misbehaviors" was present: attention-getting, power struggles, revenge, and checking out. Their teacher, at her wits' end, called me in to try to build a more respectful learning community.

My first idea was to have them work together to build a crossword puzzle of the names of their classmates. I split them into small groups, assigned rather than random, to break up cliques and to assure gender, racial, and social balance. Each child was given letter tiles for his or her name, and as a small group they were asked to build their individual letters into a crossword puzzle of their names. Some of the conversations of belonging started happening:

"Hey, we both have an *i* in our names."

"We both start with *J.*"

The following week I came back for a second session. Each child was asked to answer three sentences and share them in their small group: (1) something I am good at, (2) something I like, (3) something you don't know about me.

The next session, in their small groups, I challenged them to make a crossword puzzle of all the names of their classmates. The one rule was that the clues had to be positive (or at least neutral) descriptors of a personal attribute or characteristic.

This was by no means a fix-all solution; sometimes the interpersonal dynamics in a group can be immensely challenging, even to the most experienced of teachers. But there was a remarkable turnaround in attitudes, and increased patience with the process of building a learning community that respects differences. As to the teacher, I challenged her to give some thought to the following questions:

- *Who are these children who learn?*
- *Will their spirits feel safe in this classroom?*
- *What in their history has shaped their beliefs about themselves, their peers, their teacher and the world?*

I challenged her to also give some thought to the history that shaped her own beliefs about herself, her students, and her world. We cannot do one without the other; a respectful community is co-created when a teacher recognizes that:

Good teaching requires courage. The courage to expose one's ignorance, as well as insight, to yield some control in order to empower the group, to evoke other people's lives as well as reveal one's own.[35]

ॐ ॐ ॐ

To keep my certificate current in the state of Washington I was required to take a class for credit—any class—just to keep learning. I decided I wanted to learn to make stained-glass windows. Once I decide to do something, I don't ever start with something simple, but always like the extra challenge of making the end product functional, complex and aesthetically pleasing. As Pablo Picasso once said: "I am always doing that which I cannot do, in order that I may learn how to do it."

So I decided to make a stained-glass window to fit in the door to the parking lot of our school with the profiles of some of the children: Samantha, Bo, Jason, Courtney, Shawn, Crystal, Mara (and a few others whose names I don't remember). They sat in front of an opaque projector to cast their shadows in profile while I traced them on white butcher paper. These children were mostly all white, as the school was an alternative program in a suburb of Seattle, so

---

35. Parker J. Palmer, *Good Teaching: A Matter of Living the Mystery,* in Change Magazine (Jan/Feb 1990). Posted on www.couragerenewal.org.

I chose glass the color of the rainbow of ethnicities in the United States, ranging from African American, Latino, Native American, and Asian, from deep brown to reddish and light tan. I cut the border piece from mirror glass, to reflect the myriad of white faces in the community. All the profiles were facing one direction, looking out on the world of "white." The children often gazed at this piece of art, to find their own profile as well as to look into the mirror to see their faces reflected. They were the same children who had experimented with the *people crayons* to find a shade best matched to their skin tone.

This was another way to *build community* with a *respect for differences*. I missed the racial diversity of my New York City school, and I had just returned to this privileged school from a yearlong visiting faculty position at The Evergreen State College, teaching a coordinated studies program called Third World Focus on Early Childhood Education. Little did I know then that it was a preview of what was to come thirty-five years later, when I built the Early Learning Center in rural Uganda. *"There is a thread you follow,"* even when you don't know it.

In the last years of my paid employment as an educator I was able to combine both my interest in working with adult learners and my love of teaching children, in a role I can only describe as "chief problem solver" in a local elementary school. This position was as close to being paid to be a "resident encourager" as I could get.

か か か

Teaching as Peacemaking

If I treat my neighbor's pain and grief as foreign, I will end up suffering when my neighbor's pain and grief curdle into rage. But if I realize that in simple fact the walls between us are full of holes, I can reach through them in compassion and connection.[36]

Creating respectful communities across lines of difference is never easy. And yet holding the tensions of that challenge is what keeps me learning and engaged.

The Quakers speak of seeing that of God in each of us, of the willingness to seek that seed of the divine in everyone, even when they are your oppressor. Soon after my mother had returned from China and her experience of being held captive by the Japanese, she was living, after her repatriation, in the college town of Oberlin, Ohio. She was in need of a babysitter. My father had already returned to China.[37]

---

36. A meditation written by Rabbi Arthur Waskow on the morning after September 11, 2001.

37. Before I was born, my parents had been living and working in China during WWII. In 1943 they, along with all other Westerners living in China, were interned by the Japanese. My older brother was born in this internment camp. They were later repatriated in a prisoners-of-war exchange.

The college, knowing she had just returned from the Far East, sent her an Asian student, a young Japanese American woman. My mother took one look at her and was flooded with emotion, the memories of her suffering at the hands of her Japanese captors still quite vividly etched in her being. She visibly blanched and felt like slamming the door, but stood her ground. She somehow found the courage, the fortitude and the presence of mind to move beyond those feelings of powerlessness and was able to explain the cause of her initial double take and physical withdrawal.

The young woman, whose family had also suffered what Japanese Americans in this country experienced, had enough personal grounding and knowledge of what had transpired during the war to understand. They fell into each others' arms, with a newfound compassionate understanding of the hardships both had endured as a result of war—a moment of healing for both. As Rabbi Waskow exhorted, they courageously reached through the holes in the walls between them with compassion and connection.

ҳ҉   ҳ҉   ҳ҉

While, over the years, I have come to think of my teaching as *peacemaking*, it is more than *making peace happen*. It is my willingness to hold the possibility of peaceful solutions with grace—and faith that I can make a difference. I have always taught, regardless of the age of my students, by modeling courage, compassion, and connection—the foundations of peace: *courage* to act with integrity, *compassion* to feel another's reality, and *connection* to reach out as we, together, build bridges to peace.

ବ୍ୟ   ବ୍ୟ   ବ୍ୟ

After I left my classroom of children to work with adults in teacher education, I found that after fifteen years my stories about children were getting too old. I decided to return to the life of a school, this time as a building administrator. Much of my work as assistant principal in an elementary school was done on the playground. Some thought I was overpaid to be a "playground supervisor," but I repeatedly explained it was at the heart of my work, meeting the children on their turf. It is where I watched for "hot spots" of potential volcanic eruptions of conflict. It is where I kept my "radar" tuned to those children I knew to be volatile, children whose aggressive behavior could be sparked in a flash, children who were not yet at peace with themselves or their world.

A child would frequently come to me with a typical complaint: "Jesse's being mean..." Such a complaint could take other forms, but was usually accompanied by an expressed interest in having me in some way fix the problem, usually, in the child's mind, by punishing Jesse, or whoever the perpetrator happened to be. Invariably I would respond with: "What do you want to do about it?"

"Make him stop."

"Have you told him?"

"No."

"Let's go tell him." So we would walk over to Jesse, and I would open with: "Alice has something to tell you . . ." while prompting her: "I don't like it when . . ." letting her finish the sentence.

"I don't like it when you push me around . . ."

Again I prompted her, "And I would like you to . . ."

"And I would like you to stop."

Alice's voice gained confidence and got stronger as she began to advocate for herself. She looked up at Jesse, half expecting him to retaliate with a shove. But Jesse, typically a child without much explosive emotional baggage, was simply oblivious to the fact that his behavior was annoying to another. His response, spontaneous and genuine, "Sorry, I didn't mean to bug you, I was just playing around..."

Sometimes the perpetrator's actions were in direct retaliation or an unconscious desire for revenge for something someone else may have done. So the conflict resolution words were extended to include reciprocity, and the "I didn't like it when . . ." was followed by "Well, I didn't like it when you . . . and I will stop if you will." Mutual respect, mutual agreement—a win-win solution all around.

I could only be in so many places on the playground at one time, and it occurred to me that there was no reason why children themselves couldn't be taught this simple and respectful way of listening. So I trained a group of older students to become conflict managers, teaching them the skills of peacemaking. I used the term *conflict manager* rather than *conflict mediator*—a seemingly subtle distinction —but one that emphasized the intent of simply listening to both sides without judgment, rather than negotiating an either-or resolution. The children, ranging in age from eight to eleven, took this job very seriously. I asked them each to fill out a job application with questions about what they thought were the important qualities of a conflict manager. I was amazed at how many identified "listening to both sides" as an essential skill, how they would manage a conflict in which their best friend was involved, and what responsibilities they had outside of school, etc.

I then held a group interview, after which we brainstormed solutions to a variety of scenarios, practicing by role-playing. They also knew that a job carried responsibilities, like showing up for their shift, reporting any major issues, coming to meetings, and being role models of peacemaking rather trouble-making, problem solvers rather than problem makers, knowing that if they failed they could be fired. On the few occasions when I needed to fire someone for an infraction, it would usually only be for a few weeks and then they couldn't wait to "reapply."

What they didn't know is that I accepted any application, and silently (and sometimes overtly) encouraged students who were frequent perpetrators of violence to become conflict managers, closely monitoring the potential for abuse of power, for they were the ones most prone to wanting to "police" their peers with punitive measures, rather than build a community of respect.

ॐ　　　　ॐ　　　　ॐ

Young children like things to be black-and-white, so when asked what rules should exist in their classroom, they invariably answered:

- Don't hit people.
- Don't yell at people.
- Don't run in the halls.
- Don't push people.
- Don't take other people's stuff.
- Don't bite people.
- You should mind your own business.

The list went on and on, of all the don'ts and shoulds. I would then take the long list we generated and begin to look for the "big ideas." These always came down to three guidelines:

I. Take care of yourself.
II. Take care of each other.
III. Take care of our school (our world).

We then talked about what this might look like, inside the building, on the playground, on the bus.

One year we had a major problem on one of our busses, where the driver resorted to yelling and writing up an incident report for each child who was perceived to be out of line. Every morning I was faced with dozens of "write-ups" piled on my desk. The children arrived at school belligerent, feeling disrespected and vocally angry about what they considered unfair treatment—not an optimal way to start a day of "school" learning. So I turned the situation into an opportunity for another kind of learning, of teaching about mutual respect.

I asked the bus driver if he would be willing to stay for a few minutes at the end of his morning route (I didn't add, instead of spending the time creating "write-ups"). I gathered the children from the bus and invited them into the lunchroom where the driver was waiting. "It seems we have a problem on route number 743," I started off. "I'd like to give everyone a chance to speak about this problem, my only rule is that you have to start your sentence with 'I.'" It got real quiet.

Finally, the hand of a small eight-year-old girl sitting in the back went up.

"I think it is too noisy on the bus." Her comment broke the group's initial silence. Nods all around, including from the driver.

A boy, who usually sat in the back of the bus volunteered, "I don't like it when kids change seats when they are not supposed to." More nods from the driver.

"I don't like it when the driver yells at us."

"I feel bad because the driver doesn't know my name, like I don't exist."

The driver then spoke up: "I can't drive safely when it is noisy and you kids are out of your seats. When I have to turn around to tell you to stop, I can't look at the traffic. That scares me so I get mad; I don't want to yell, but I don't know what else to do."

It got real quiet. I continued to simply listen.

"Yeah, guys! You don't want us to crash, do you?" piped up a lively six-year-old.

"What can we do about it?" was all I asked, and I was flooded with the group's ideas, recording them on a chalkboard. The only direction I gave was that we were looking for solutions for the future, not blame or punishment for the past. We came up with a list of agreements they could all live with, which included staying in their seats and the driver learning their names. They each, the driver included, simply wanted to be heard, to be seen, to know they would be taken seriously, to know that someone cared about how they felt. The whole thing took about twenty minutes and while I can't truthfully say that #743 became a model bus, we certainly had children arriving at school calmer and eager to learn, and a driver grateful for a busload of much more self-controlled charges, who suddenly became "real" children to him. Teaching is about becoming "real" to one another.

そ   そ   そ

Chapter Four

Teaching and Beyond

There is a thread you follow. It goes among
things that change. But it doesn't change . . .
—William Stafford

In 2007, when I moved on from my school administration position, I had very little idea of what I would do in retirement. I decided to keep up my connections with children by volunteering to be a guardian ad litem, a court-appointed special advocate for children in foster care (CASA). It would be one way for me to continue to "speak up for a child." I also felt the pull to revisit West Africa, where I had spent a summer while in college, and where my father had spent considerable time during my youth in Geneva. There was a certain joy about my father's being, an unspoken exuberance whenever he returned from his trips to Africa. His enthusiasm certainly rubbed off on me. While talking to a friend, I mentioned that I was looking for a way of returning to Africa.

She reconnected me with one of my former graduate students who was heading up an organization to help build capacity in schools in rural Uganda. This was not West Africa, but nonetheless I was interested in finding out more.

I called her up, and she immediately asked when I could go. So in July 2009 I took my first trip to Uganda. I was immediately put to work at the small private elementary school where her organization was helping to build a new classroom block: leading staff meetings, interviewing students, teachers, parents—certainly more than I bargained for as a mere volunteer. While there I met a local educator named Jane, the head teacher for another primary school in the area, this one a government-funded school. "My dream," Jane told me as we walked down the dusty dirt road, "is to start an Early Childhood Center . . ." In her small rural community there were no programs for children under age six.

I was intrigued and returned to Uganda in March 2010 with the intent of continuing that conversation. But Jane, a woman of both vision and action, didn't just simply dream about it, she went and did it: moved out of her house into a different structure on her land, and opened the doors of what had been her living room to young children ages three to seven. She expected she would start with fifteen to twenty children, but when I arrived a month after the school had started, there were already thirty-five enrolled, crammed into a space twelve feet long and six feet wide. Five benches in a row, each held seven little bodies, cheek to cheek, eagerly listening to their teacher. When they needed to write or draw on their slate chalkboards, they knelt on the dirt floor and used the benches as tables. Jane named the school JEBMIDH, each letter the first initial of her six children, and the last letter *H* for *hope.* The motto of the school became *Nezikoolima gaali magi* in Luganda meaning, "Even crowing roosters were once eggs."

I was so touched by the sight of these children crammed into this tiny space that I asked Jane what she most needed. "I need to build a building . . . I have the land, but we need a building." I don't know what possessed me, but I responded immediately, "Let me see what I can do . . ." not knowing how I could be of much help. I came back to the United States and started a "Brick-by-Brick" campaign among friends and family, with a goal of eight thousand bricks, a figure I pulled out of the air at random. At a dollar a brick, I could make a dent in funding this project. Never before in my life had I raised money for much of anything; I had, in fact, always run the other way if I was asked to serve on a board of directors that involved fund-raising. Somehow money began pouring in, fueled by my passion and my convincing clarity of why I was embarking on building a preschool in rural Uganda.

When I returned to Uganda in February 2011, there were ninety students enrolled, and we began planning in earnest: sketching floor plans, roughing out a budget, keeping current on the price of cement and mud bricks. In December of the same year we broke ground, and now have a brand-new three-classroom building, completed in the spring of 2012, with a rain catchment system to provide cleaner drinking water than what is usually collected from the borehole shared with cattle.

Nothing in rural sub-Saharan Africa is easy, and the process of construction was an eye-opener for me. The following is a letter written after my December 2011 visit to all those who made a contribution to this project.

December 18, 2011

A glimpse into construction in rural Uganda...

My hope was that construction would start immediately upon my arrival on Thanksgiving Day. However, nothing in Uganda, especially in rural areas, happens with anything resembling immediacy. Patience, I told myself. And yet my privileged Western impatience sometimes got the better of me, as I began to understand and relax into a very different reality.

Our first problem was the delivery of materials, for we were at the end of the rainy season, the ground was soft, and the roads, rivers of mud, making a truck delivery of sand and gravel impossible.

We had to wait for a few dry days.

In the meantime, a girl at school had been bitten by a poisonous snake. We dropped everything to transport her to the nearest clinic, eight kilometers away, on the back of the first available "b o d a - b o d a ,"
Uganda's motorcycle version of a taxi, for no one has private cars. The next day was the last day of the school year at the elementary school, and one hundred parents and grandparents had assembled to take part in festivities, which included singing and dancing by each age group and many long-winded speeches by various dignitaries, a large spread of local dishes, and a three-hour auction of various crafts made by students. I bid on a basket and a mat, both woven by children. We were there well after dark.

The next day, we took the students on a field trip to the nearest village of Kassanda, piling all of them in the back of a lorry. They each stood and none fell out, singing at the top of their lungs the JEBMIDH theme song: "We are bright, we are bright—the children of JEBMIDH" as we barreled along, bumping over the one-lane deeply eroded dirt road, barely as wide as the

109 ࣸ

truck. We had packed drums to play, a few balls, and a huge kettle of cooked rice for lunch. We efficiently kept the meal warm for several hours by wrapping the kettle in the ubiquitous banana leaves. We visited the clinic, the police station, a carpenter's workshop, the credit union bank, a storefront shop, a fuel station, and the public taxi park. The children had been prepped and could read the words "nurse," "clinic," "bank," "police man," "carpenter," etc.—language experience at its very best, reminding me of my earliest days in New York City on field trips with the same age group. These young children are such eager learners they soaked it all up.

We were finally ready to start construction. Jane had arranged for a crew of three builders, along with her brother, Uncle Willy, who supervised the work. I soon discovered that while they were professional builders, they were not contractors, and expected all materials and tools to be on location. So, along with all her other responsibilities, Jane was now ordering bags of cement, and checking on other deliveries, as well as walking forty-five minutes to check on the quality of stones to be delivered. Since no shop delivered, transport had to be arranged separately. Jane's cell phone ran out of airtime and her second phone had a dead battery and couldn't be charged until she got to town, but the power there had been out for over a week. She used my phone that mercifully still had both juice and airtime. So much that I took for granted. Nothing is ever easy in rural Uganda.

Jane's phone rang late in the night.[38] It was Katumba, the head builder, asking for funds to be sent by "mobile money" (using a cell phone account to wire money), for he couldn't get to the work site without money to pay for transportation. However, his cell phone fell into a latrine, and we waited another day for him to secure another phone.

Finally they arrived, each with a blanket and a change of clothes: they would sleep on the floor of Jane's living room, on one foam mattress turned sideways as a pillow to accommodate all three of them. Room and board were included in their costs because they would be living at Jane's for the duration of the project. After a delivery of fifty bags of cement, also to be stored in Jane's living room—protection from the rain and theft— the three of them moved into a shed behind the outdoor kitchen area.

The first step was clearing the land. Everyone helped: children, neighbors, paid builders, and day laborers,

---

38. In Uganda only outgoing calls require airtime. Incoming calls are free.

for clearing the land, like everything else, was done by hand, with the help of a few hoes, a rake, a slasher, a saw. Trees were uprooted and cut, sticks were collected and carried back to Jane's kitchen for firewood. Katumba scoped out the site, while one of his crew cut pickets to hold the marking string. I watched with interest as he checked the ninety-degree angle of his corner with the help of Pythagoras's theorem. He didn't need a square. A plumb line and a hammer were the only tools he brought with him. The foundation was dug by hand as well, using a simple hoe. It was beginning to take shape. Local tradition demanded that a rooster be killed, and its blood and feathers spread in the foundation. I was impressed with Katumba; he was smart, knowledgeable, conscientious, and honest. Uncle Willy kept meticulous records of deliveries made, materials used and daily achievements.

Cement was also mixed by hand. Water had to be hauled from the borehole about a quarter of a mile away. Saulo and Joshua, both fifteen, did this by strapping four or five jerry cans of water on a bicycle and wheeling it up the road. They had already made sixty trips for water by the day I left. Construction should be completed by early spring if we don't run into any snags with materials availability and delivery, some needing to come from Kampala, the capital city some three hours away, and some available locally, meaning the village of Kassanda.

I was really in awe of all that we had accomplished in these past two weeks, bringing to reality what was a dream we have shared. Parents in Kassanda, who had no preschool option in their own community, were now talking of organizing a bus to bring their children out to JEBMIDH. Our school had rapidly gained a reputation in central Uganda for quality, high standards, care, and best practices in Early Childhood Education. I will continue to do my part, and hope you will continue to support the nurturing of this small miracle in whatever way you can.

With gratitude, Jeanne

          ॐ   ॐ   ॐ

More than a small miracle took place, for I had no idea when I simply said, "Let me see what I can do . . ." that I would successfully raise funds, and that the community would so soon have a real early learning center, and one being recognized for its excellence.

This beautiful, new school building now stands as a beacon of hope in this rural Ugandan community. Ninety-some children, ages three to eight, arrive early in the morning, rain or shine, eager and ready to learn. Thinking about them at the start of each day just makes me smile. Moving into the new building happened in late spring 2012—everyone joined in!

Since I was not able to stay for the duration of the construction project, I hired one of Jane's sons as the official photographer. He sent me this photo, taken with his cell phone.

While schools in Uganda historically use an antiquated sixty-year-old British colonial model (teacher-directed call-and-response), the three young teachers at JEBMIDH Infant School are also learning about child development and are beginning to focus on the whole child, incorporating such notions as curiosity, self-reliance, interdependence, and integrated, experiential learning. During each of my five visits to the school I spent time helping these young teachers expand their knowledge and understanding of how young children learn.

I never once thought, at least consciously, that in retirement I would be building a school in a remote area of Uganda. I remember my childhood decision to teach kindergarten in Africa. Who knew it would take me a lifetime of teaching and learning to call me back to that early leading? Now I am not just teaching kindergarteners, but their teachers as well. *"There is a thread you follow. It goes among things that change, but it doesn't change . . ."* Into that thread I have woven my own experiences, and my yearning for the world to truly become *us*.

Chapter Five

To Be of Service

If we are to reach real peace in the world,
we shall have to begin with the children.
—Gandhi

How and when did I decide to become a teacher? I always asked that same question of my graduate students. Their responses invariably fell into one of three categories:

- "I always knew I wanted to be a teacher."
- "I came into teaching quite by accident . . ."
- "After I had children of my own, I got curious about how they learn, and was hooked."

I fell into the first category; I always knew I wanted to be a teacher. I was not one of those children who loved to gather her friends to "play school." But from as young as seven or eight years old, I often observed younger children; I paid attention to what they said and did. Perhaps even then young children were, to me, more real, more accessible than the adults I encountered.

I don't come from a family of educators, and yet both of my parents, as well as my grandfather, Tracy, were important teachers who instilled in me a curiosity about the world. More than curiosity, they modeled for me a life of service. I wanted to make a difference. They taught me to be resilient even in the face of adversity. They connected me to something larger than myself, a larger story. My uncle, at ninety-seven, recently wrote in his autobiography: "In everything I have done, my family's values have always held up. We were taught to always look on the best side of things, to believe the best about people, no matter where they came from, to meet each challenge as part of life."[39]

He, too, was one of the adults in my life who

inspired me to go beyond, to think big, to see the world from all sides, inside and out . . . to "make the world a better place" . . . I'm from big shoes to fill and making my own footprints.

The call to be of service runs deep in my veins, from generations of compassionate and passionate individuals with generous hearts and kind speech, who want to make the world a better place. In my own way I have filled (and continue to fill) those big shoes. I have also made my own footprints, on paths of my own making, holding on to that sometimes-elusive *thread I follow.*

---

39. Tracy Strong Jr., *The Better Part of a Century* (2013), 179.

Resilience
and the Importance of Story

I have often asked myself why some children, against all odds, seem not only to survive but also to thrive, while others, faced with similar adversities, seem to struggle or even crumble. What makes that difference? As *one* teacher at a critical juncture in a child's life, I can make a difference — but there is more. I am thinking of a number of children I have known, living with poverty, hunger, violence, alcoholism, abandonment, who would go on to become leaders in their communities. Is resilience something children are born with?

Mikeh (the one who wanted to know if his skin would turn white if he came to A-me-ri-ka), was brought by his mother at age five to visit a distant cousin who lived in a rural part of his native Uganda. He was to spend a few weeks there. His mother then simply disappeared and never returned. Seven years later, Mikeh was still living with this relative. He was at the top of his class in school. He had the responsibility to care for the family's herd of cattle. Why wasn't he traumatized by his abandonment? How did he learn to thrive? He became a part of a larger family, connected to the larger clan that included his wayward mother. He had a place, a role as a valued contributing member of the extended family. Despite all odds, he turned into a bright, outgoing young man with an insatiable curiosity about the world.

∾ ∾ ∾

In my role as "resident encourager," I often worked with students, many of them students of color and/or poverty, who were struggling academically, not so much because they didn't have the intellectual capacity for success, but because they didn't have confidence in themselves and didn't trust that anyone believed in them. They didn't feel they belonged, or mattered. I started asking them as a group what they were curious about, what they wondered about. They struggled with this question, and got only as far as saying things like, "I wonder what's for lunch..." Freedom of imagination is a luxury not afforded to children who know only survival mode. Yet that single orientation to intellectual curiosity, so familiar to most children from white middle-class professional families, can mark the difference in academic achievement. The luxury of being curious about the world comes from knowing, like Mikeh, that you belong to something larger, even if your immediate family has struggles. It comes from a sense of connection.

∾ ∾ ∾

Marshall Duke, a psychologist at Emory University, and Robyn Fivush, the director of Emory's Family Narrative Lab,[40] found that children who knew the most about their families tended to be the most resilient in the face of adversity. They discovered, through asking a set of questions about family stories, that children who know their family history, stories of their parents' and grandparents' struggles and triumphs, challenges and idiosyncrasies, had a stronger sense of their intergenerational selves, their connection not just to their parents, but to previous generations as well. They were better able to meet challenges as they arose because of their strong sense of belonging to something bigger than themselves.

I found that many children in Uganda, despite all odds, have a deep sense of belonging to something larger than themselves, knowing they will be cared for, and that they have a place, a role in the larger clan. I watched Nantaba, age two, explore her world, and in the week I stayed with her extended family, I never could figure out who her biological mother was, because she was cared for in community.

I watched Jackson, his green checked shirt, mis-buttoned with the one remaining button, hung loosely on his small, wiry body. His deep chocolate smooth skin shone. He looked up at me warily. Two new front teeth filled a gap, perfectly straight, perfectly white, though they have never seen a toothbrush or the ubiquitous *Col-ga-te*, as it is pronounced

---

40. Marshall Duke and Robyn Fivush, "The Stories That Bind Us". *The Huffington Post* (April 28, 2013).

in Uganda. He smiled, unsure of the whiteness of my skin. His eyes darted down, "Good morning, Madam," the words automatically flew from his mouth, though I heard a silent *muzungu, muzungu,* a word that is always filled with a bit of wonderment.[41] His eyes, big and curious, peered cautiously at me. I guessed he was about seven, judging from his new front teeth, though when I inquired he was not sure. Birthdays are rarely acknowledged in Uganda. He lived at the school, and wanted to be a teacher when he grew up. He lived at the school because what was left of his immediate family lived too far away for him to walk every day. His parents were both dead of AIDS.

So what is it like to be him? What is it like to know only the small hut where he sleeps with eleven other boys, the mud brick structure that houses the school? What images go through his mind? I watched him and Mikeh slaughter a chicken—knowing exactly where and how to kill it without causing undue suffering—knowing exactly where and how to dunk it in heated water and for how long before plucking the feathers off. I watched him as he expertly butchered it into pieces for the cooking pot. Each child in this small Ugandan rural community has a role, a purpose, and responsibilities. Jackson knows he belongs. Not every child in the world feels that sense of importance and belonging.

A sense of belonging comes when you know that someone has seen you; that you matter, that you belong to a larger

---

41. An African term used to describe people of European descent. It is also often equated with wealth, knowledge and power.

community. That community lays the groundwork for resilience.

❧   ❧   ❧

A number of years ago our family gathered for my parents' fiftieth wedding anniversary. My father, proud of his three children's involvement in higher education, decided we would hold daily "seminars" to share whatever we each were working on. As a teacher educator, I shared what was most important to me: that my students know where they had come from, what had shaped their values, so that they in turn might be more open to understanding where their students had come from.

I gathered all the grandchildren, ranging in age from five to eighteen, to interview their grandparents, for it was important to me that my children and my brothers' children also know where they came from. I worked with the children to craft their questions and my "seminar" contribution was these interviews. Stories I had never heard before came out of my parents.

"Grandpa, were you ever naughty?"

"Grandma, did you ever lie?"

"Grandpa, how do you think growing up today is different from when you grew up?"

"Grandma, what are you most proud of?"

The range of questions mirrored the developmental stages of these five- to-eighteen-year-olds.

The five younger cousins, ranging in age from five to eleven, then decided to put on a seventeen-scene play in four acts of all the stories they had heard about their parents and grandparents, starting with their grandfather being mean to his younger brother; on to their grandmother playing "hooky" from school; to her near death after the birth of their uncle John; to her tears over the possibility of her lost passport being sold on the black market; to when their uncle Tracy first got glasses; and to their parents playing endless games of kick the can. There was no question they each had a strong sense of their intergenerational selves and that they belonged to something larger than themselves.

Years later, in my work with teachers, I started using the "Where I'm From" activity, for it offers an important opportunity to revisit those connections, to claim or reclaim, as Mary Oliver puts it in her poem *Wild Geese,* "your place in the family of things."[42]

                                                                                ॐ   ॐ   ॐ

---

42. Mary Oliver, *New and Selected Poems* (Boston, MA: Beacon Press, 1992), 110.

One More Lesson: Humility
What Help Is Helpful?

Being of service also has a shadow side, for I need to pay attention to my intentions, my motivation. My *service* may not be needed, and may not even be helpful. If I am not careful, what seem like good intentions may simply be self-serving. Despite all my efforts to listen and not make assumptions: to instill in children a sense of self-reliance, competence, and self-confidence; to empower them to take charge of their own lives, I often find myself walking a fine line between "guiding" and "doing for."

When my children were young, my mother watched my youngest son struggle to tie his shoes. She wanted to take over and do it for him. I made a pointed remark about how in this house, we wait until asked before assuming help is needed or wanted. Even in her later years, she frequently remarked on the lesson she had learned from my comment. As an extraordinarily competent and accomplished woman, she sometimes had areas of blindness that didn't allow her to appreciate that her need to do for another came from her need to control, and often resulted in the undermining of another's self-confidence. I remember one year during a visit with my parents, my children had requested lasagna for dinner. I set about to first cook the pasta. As I removed each wide noodle from the boiling water to let it drain and cool before building the dish, my mother repositioned every single noodle. I pointed out how her actions made me feel there was something wrong with what I had done. "I was only trying to help . . ." she retorted. I am my mother's daughter. Sometimes my need to help is merely controlling, disguised as good intentions. Sometimes my need to help is merely a projection based on my own needs, my own perceptions.

So advocating for a child, speaking up for a child, inviting their voice to be heard must go hand in hand with empowering. When does "advocating for" become disempowering? I am reminded of a Ugandan friend who, feeling that Ben's English was hard for me to understand, reiterated everything Ben said and answered for him, even though Ben and I had understood one another perfectly. Ben, frustrated, became silent, and less confident of his English. While my friend thought he was being helpful, his help, in fact, was disempowering.

☙   ☙   ☙

When I was in teacher education, in one of my seminars I always led a discussion of *Power On, Power For,* and *Power With* and the role of the authority of a teacher. We looked at models of teacher-child relationships in the context of a classroom:

- *Power On*: in which the teacher assumes an authoritarian role in a vertical relationship of power, and in which the child has no or little sense of voice;
- *Power For*: in which the teacher has abdicated responsibility for authority and gives over to the demands of the child;
- *Power With*: in which teacher and student share both power and responsibility.

In my work with classroom teachers in Positive Discipline, we called these structural frameworks the "authoritarian," the "permissive," and the "democratic" classrooms.

I always reminded my teachers and graduate students to remember that in advocating for children, in speaking up for a child, there is always a danger of being too helpful, of disempowering rather than empowering. How do they support a child's developing sense of competence as they gauge their own desire to be helpful? And I continue to ask myself how can I be of service without "fixing"?

Rachel Naomi Remen, in an article entitled, "Helping, Fixing or Serving?" writes:

In fixing we see others as broken, and respond to this perception with our expertise. Fixers trust their own expertise but may not see the wholeness in another person or trust the integrity of the life in them. When we serve, we see and trust that wholeness. We respond to it and collaborate with it. And when we see the wholeness in another, we strengthen it.

They may then be able to see it for themselves for the first time.[43]

❧   ❧   ❧

Before my first trip to Uganda, I asked a colleague what gifts I should bring. Pot holders . . . clothespins . . . were a few of the items she mentioned. I know she meant well, but sometimes help comes in the form of pure projection. Her perception was based solely on her own experience. No doubt her preconceived idea of hanging clothes to dry mandated clothespins, and she would have wanted a pot holder to handle a pan on an open fire. I felt rather foolish when I gave Ben wooden clothespins to give to his wife. They did not use them. I further exacerbated the situation by asking why. He obliged out of respect—and because I was a visitor, and I came from a country of wealth and knowledge. There is still a cultural perception that whites know better.

I am reminded of another young Ugandan friend who was teaching a class on sanitation, hygiene, and clean water in his village. The participants, while they were receptive to the information, all wanted to know where the *muzungu* was, discounting his expertise because no white person was in charge. Residual attitudes from colonial days are still so thoroughly ingrained in the very fabric of the culture.

---

43. Rachel Naomi Remen, "Helping, Fixing or Serving?" *Shambhala Sun* (September 1999).

Not only are residual elements of white power and privilege ingrained into this postcolonial culture, but those attitudes mirror my own assumptions. Internalized oppression goes hand in hand with internalized superiority, reinforcing each other, so that often without thinking I assume *my* way is the *right* way. That first lesson I learned in teaching, about *checking my assumptions* is never far from the surface.

On my next visit to Uganda, even though pot holders were again suggested, I didn't take any. I thought I would rather observe what was needed than make assumptions based on my own preconceived ideas. As I sat with my friend Jane, at the fire, as she cooked our next meal, I watched her pick up a pot out of the flames of the wood fire with her bare hands. I watched her pick up a coal from the fire to place it in the ironing box. She had no need of a pot holder!

Sometimes the perceived need for help is pure projection of our own needs, for I would have wanted to use a pot holder. My hands aren't toughened like Jane's, so my needs are different. Jane teased me about my wimpy hands—and they are by no means delicate—when I was helping her remove the dried corn kernels from the cob so that they could be ground into flour. The action required a twisting, wringing motion, and within minutes I had worked up a large blister at the base of my thumb.

I wondered why Jane insisted on ironing *all* my clothes, even my undergarments. An iron in a remote region without electricity is little more than an old-fashioned coal box, with embers heating a triangular-shaped plate. Banana leaves provide steam if needed, or cool the iron if too hot. I usually try to avoid any ironing, but she explained the reason: since the clothes are washed in cold water drawn from a borehole shared with cattle and other critters, ironing killed any residual bacteria. It is only by being exposed to a different way that we can learn to question our assumptions. Sometimes my own perceptions and habits mask the possibility of wisdom I don't yet have.

I watched Sam as he prepared eggs for breakfast. He planned to scramble them, so he poked a small hole at the tip of the shell by tapping it with the point of a sharp knife, much as I would do were I trying to preserve the shell. He shook out the contents. I wanted to demonstrate how "we" crack eggs in America, so I took a knife to crack the shell in the center. Just as the blade came down, I suddenly realized two things simultaneously. The first was that these eggs, unlike our store-bought ones, had not been washed, and I was therefore introducing a host of bacteria into the egg matter. The other realization was that what the Ugandans call *local eggs*, collected from truly free-range chickens, might be more than just fertile, since there was no way of knowing when the egg had been laid. Who was I to assume I knew a better way to crack an egg?

On the London Underground there is a wonderful reminder: *MIND THE GAP* . . . repeated endlessly, as the train doors close. To me, this simple statement carries much larger implications, reminding me once again to *stop . . . look . . . and listen*; to pay attention, to check my assumptions, for my way may not be "The Way" for all. I need to practice what Parker Palmer calls an *appreciation of otherness.* He describes in his book, *Healing the Heart of Democracy,* one of the five habits of the heart:

> *developing an appreciation of otherness, it is by crossing lines of difference in my life that I can become a larger person, that I learn I have more to learn from those who are different from me than I do from those who are like me. And when you walk across those lines of difference—and start discovering that the world is a larger place and a much more interesting place than you knew, you can become larger in yourself—and you become more at home on the face of this earth.[44]*

My work in Uganda clearly takes me across lines of difference. With humility, I learn to see the world from multiple perspectives, and recognize "the world into which I was born is just one model of reality..."[45]

చ చ చ

---

44. From an interview with Parker Palmer on "The Five Habits of the Heart," from his book *Healing the Heart of Democracy* (San Francisco: CA: Jossey-Bass, 2011) 43-46.

45. Wade Davis, from a poster published by the Syracuse Cultural Workers, 2003.

When does helping across lines of class and color, culture and language transgress to become patronizing or imperialistic? Sometimes those of us who were born into power and privilege forget that our help is not always welcome. These questions arose early on for me, though I didn't understand it at the time. My father, while initially convinced that the Church had answers for all the ills of the world, soon became disillusioned and realized that the cumbersomeness of the institution of mission and church proved to be an impediment to building relationships across lines of difference. He came to deeply understand that he could no longer work under the American Board of Missions, because he felt that to live true to the Social Gospel and never violate the identity and integrity of another human being, he should not be trying to convince or convert others to his worldview. Rather, his job as a missionary was to seek to understand other worldviews—not a commonly held perspective in 1945— but one that certainly was in keeping with his own family's values, and with what he believed it meant to be a Christian, to "love thy neighbor as thyself."[46] He learned that help is not always helpful. My father wrote of our reasons for finally leaving Communist China to head to Korea, despite his desire to stay and be of service: "We were becoming an embarrassment and a handicap to our Chinese colleagues. . ." Our help was no longer helpful.

---

46. Mark 12:31.

Dambisa Moyo, a Zambian economist, writes in *Dead Aid,* why aid to African countries doesn't work and is, in fact, detrimental to establishing self-sufficiency. She points out that all the free aid has brought about a handout mentality that has destroyed incentives for change, and has further pushed a fragile economy into a downward spiral of further poverty. She points out that donors from wealth complain of lack of visible progress,[47] and continue to try to help "those poor people," by "doing for," but more often to feel that they have tried to do some "good" as defined in their own cultural framework. When help creates dependency, it is no longer helpful. For real change to take root, *power with* is required, a shared investment of responsibility and ownership.

After my first trip to Uganda I wrote the following article, based on something that really happened, to remind myself of how my work there had the potential to create dependency rather than autonomy and self-empowerment.

What Takes Root

A number of years ago, two different European NGOs became interested in "helping" a primary school in a community of rural Uganda. They decided what the school needed most was a new building. So they started with traditional mud bricks, amazed at how easy the job would be. However, in their haste, the bricks were not properly cured, and the building, now housing two

---

47. Dambisa Moyo, *Dead Aid* (New York, NY: Farrar, Strauss and Giroux, 2009).

classrooms, shook every time the wind blew. The building has now fallen down to a rubble of bricks. Fortunately, no child was injured.

The other NGO took a little more time and thought before starting a new classroom building, though they had never physically spent any time in Uganda or at the school. They simply wanted to do "good" in a part of the world that has very little monetary resources by donating funds to finish the project. Their funds dried up, and the sturdy half-built walls stand four feet tall, sheltering only weeds.

These well-meaning NGOs, however, did make a positive lasting contribution: they planted three mango trees. These trees took root, and now stand tall, gracing the school grounds, providing much needed shade, as well as fruit to feed the children.

What takes root is what comes from the African soil, from the local community, from meeting the needs of the children and their families. What will grow and last comes from the people, not what well-meaning outsiders think they need. This means listening and learning from the local people, finding out what a school community needs by spending time on-site, forming a true partnership that embraces and celebrates the local community, its children and families.

The metaphor of these three mango trees reminds us that what takes root must start in the local community, and that donor funds, when they disappear, leave only disappointment and half-finished buildings. The JEBMIDH

Infant School has taken root in the local community, locally owned, locally run, and self-sustaining.

When the construction of our three-classroom building was completed, Jane showed me construction plans for three additional classrooms, a library, an administration building, and staff quarters—a worthy, albeit ambitious endeavor. I had the difficult task of reiterating to Jane my commitment to the three-classroom building, but, as a single individual whose training and interests are more with teacher development than funding development, I had exhausted my resources. There is always the risk that *help* will create dependency, and dependency only perpetuates a "handout-from-donor" mindset, a form of colonialism, a deep divide of privilege between the "haves" and the "have-nots," attitudes that have often been internalized. Just as I was acutely aware in watching Sam crack the eggs, internalized perception of entitlement runs deep, both for "haves" and "have-nots," and both—often unconsciously—participate in perpetuating that divide.

Jane, of course, was disappointed, but I also realized I was walking a fine line between making it possible for her to follow her dream, and creating donor dependency. I pointed out to her, after a close look at the budget, that if she were more diligent about collecting school fees, she could gradually save enough to continue her own construction, emphasizing that all along I have been clear that the project needs to be self-sustaining. In a phone call upon my return to the United

States, when we discussed the height of the new tables and chairs to be built by a local carpenter, she enthusiastically told me of her plans to write more children's books, perhaps even in local language, inspired by my *Alphabet Book*. Her comment was: "It is time for me to write my own books, I can do this . . ." I heard in that statement echoes of my challenge to move to self-reliance. I have no doubt that someday she will realize the second part of her dream: to create a demonstration Lab School for training early childhood educators! And that is as it should be: a local affair.

ঽ   ঽ   ঽ

Last year, Godfrey, an aspiring young Ugandan apprentice teacher, had become frustrated with one of his students, and was heavy-handed with him, leaving a mark on his neck. The boy's father was irate and very ready to take "matters into his own hands," threatening to do bodily harm to the young teacher. My friend Joseph intervened and calmed the father by reassuring him the matter would be resolved by the school's administration, and Godfrey would be duly disciplined. Joseph came to me to ask me to talk to Godfrey. I refused. As a *muzungu,* moreover, a *muzungu woman*, my presence would only shame Godfrey and discourage and secretly anger him.

I suggested to Joseph that he tell Godfrey that he understood how much this young boy had challenged his authority (tenuous at best, but don't tell him that), and that the boy's father wanted to kill him. Joseph agreed to help him look for solutions for what to do when a student challenged his authority, without resorting to corporal punishment.

I watched as Joseph gathered Godfrey with the school's owner/director and Margaret, a teacher with considerable experience. They sat under the mango tree for close to half an hour. I could feel some of the tension relax, as I observed from across the playfield. When they broke up, Joseph came to me and thanked me. "I said exactly what you told me to," and what was so amazing is that the older teacher sympathized with Godfrey's position, and offered to work with him to find alternative solutions—the best of all worlds, for now the resources lay not in the hands of the outside experts— nor in the hands of a *muzungu* woman, but in the hands of local colleagues.

It was an invaluable lesson I won't soon forget. I am acutely aware of the cultural overlay—and the weight carried by the whiteness of my skin. My assumption of privilege (and the assumption of most people who look like me) is so prevalent, and a cautious reminder to one who is asking, "What help is helpful?" The sentiments of Lao Tzu echo:

> *Go to the people. Learn from them. Live with them. Love them. Start with what they know. Build with what they have . . .*

What help is helpful? Or: when is help helpful? I keep learning . . . My efforts to help Miriam, a bright and talented Ugandan girl are part of my lessons.

As we started down to the watering hole on my first evening in rural Uganda, Miriam caught up with me, and unlike her peers, initiated a conversation and introduced herself. She carried a five-gallon jerry can, or "jelly" can, as they are known in Ugandan English. She spoke with ease, comfortable in conversation. She informed me she was fourteen years old, that her favorite subject in school was science; that she was in P-7 (Primary Seven), the last year in the primary education system. I asked her of her future schooling plans. "I want to be a doctor," she informed me. I could discern curious ears among the other girls, who were slightly in awe of her, as she was the "Head Girl" at school. She also had the responsibility for making sure enough water was brought up to the kitchen area each evening. Her charges, ten girls between the ages of six and twelve, proceeded down to the watering hole, a muddy pond about twelve feet across, surrounded by cattle prints.

Miriam watched as the children, in pairs, knelt down on logs strategically placed to allow access to deeper water without standing in mud. They used their jerry cans to displace the surface scum, before submersing the yellow containers and waiting for them to fill. Miriam went last, and then before hoisting her can to her head, helped the younger ones lift theirs, first to a shoulder, and then to their heads. I tried to lift one, but could hardly get it off the ground, much less hoist it to my shoulder. The children laughed at my efforts. Each child's technique differed a little, some supported with one hand, some with elbows forming a triangular platform. The only one hands-free, Miriam led the way back up the hill with the jerry can perfectly balanced on her head.

Photo by Ken Driese

Later that evening, we gathered inside and the children performed songs and dances, with Miriam taking the lead singing role, in a call-and-response, as is the custom. "AIDS... AIDS... Our people are dying...What are we going to do?" she sang out with confidence. I was moved not only by the content of the song, but by her presence, her poise, her musicianship, and her leadership.

When I returned to visit eight months later, Miriam had finished primary school, doing fairly well in the exit exams. I asked her guardian where she was in secondary school.

"She is not in school, there is no money..." I discovered, much to my dismay. I asked what it would take to get her in school. About $120 . . . I made an agreement with her guardian that I would take care of school fees, if he would cover other expenses. In hindsight, I wonder if she wasn't in school simply because he figured I would come up with the needed money. Two days later she was in school, boarding at a secondary school owned by a friend of her guardian's.

I went to visit Miriam at her school at the beginning of her second year. I found her looking drawn, frightened, and almost in tears. She did tell me she wanted to take a computer class, but that cost more. I agreed to make sure that would happen. I asked her about the school's music program. There wasn't one. Music was one of the realms where she could shine, regain her poise and confidence, but this school offered no such program. I know the decision to send her to that school was purely based on her guardian's friendship with its owner, not on Miriam's best interest. In my haste to be helpful, I had helped her to be placed in a school ill matched to her needs.

When is help helpful? What responsibility did I have to make it right? I contacted her guardian and expressed my concern over Miriam's placement, and much to my surprise he said they would look for another school. In my last visit with Miriam in September 2012 in her new school, she expressed her gratitude to me for the change. I remain cautiously optimistic, while realizing that my "help" from afar can sometimes make life more difficult. In the end, my "help" in this case seems to have been helpful.

ॐ   ॐ   ॐ

I recently became aware of a unique opportunity for sub-Saharan youth to study for a university degree in the United States, provided they qualified academically, are without financial means, and are committed to returning to their home country to serve.

I immediately sent the information off to David, a bright and dedicated young Ugandan man determined to bring health care to remote areas of Uganda. The first place he applied asked for his social security number, his SAT scores, and his bank account number. Mystified, he e-mailed me from his cell phone, wondering what all that was about. It turns out he had applied to the Health Sciences program, as it was the first one listed at the American University of Beirut. Nothing on the website indicated that that program was designed only for students from other Arab nations. So I directed him to the participating universities in the United States.

The next question came within a few hours: an application fee was required. I sent him more information on how to get it waived. He still was accessing all the information from his cell phone, and successfully sent off his completed application.

The next day brought another discouraging message: "They now want my TOEFL scores."[48]

This young man, however, not to be deterred, was quite resourceful and learned that this English proficiency exam was offered at the U.S. Embassy in the capital city. In addition, the British version was offered at the British Consulate. Both would be offered on February 14. The application deadline was February 15. More bad news came with his research: the cost of either test was around $200. I was momentarily tempted to just send him the funds and be done with it, but realized in so doing I would not be doing him a favor, nor would I help to change a system that seemed less than "user friendly" to any student from a developing country. I had learned something about what help is helpful. Instead, realizing how much easier it was for me to do some research—given easy Internet access and a similar time zone—I sent him the contact information for an admissions counselor. He immediately corresponded directly with the university counselor, who told him that unfortunately his scores would not be received in time for the deadline, and she could therefore not consider his application for the coming school year.

David and I exchanged the following e-mails.

I wrote:
I too am disappointed that they are not able to extend the deadline and make an exception by accepting late test scores, but I understand from my conversations

---

48. TOEFL stands for Test of English as a Foreign Language.

with both Dr. A. and Dr. J. that they have many many applicants, far too many to make exceptions. It is unfortunate that I didn't know about this opportunity sooner. I am greatly admiring of how well you were able to secure the necessary information in such a short amount of time. You are very resourceful and will go far!

The good news is that the opportunity will still be there, and by all means you should apply for the following year. This will also give you an opportunity to explore some of the other universities, and I would encourage you to apply to more than one university. (Young people in the U.S., when they are ready to apply to university, always apply to several different places, in case they are not accepted at their first or second choices.)

Whenever I receive disappointing news, I always try to look at what I can learn from the situation. I believe you have already learned so much just from having gotten this far in the process, and you have learned that large organizations in the United States usually stand by the policies they have put in place—and I respect that, for they cannot be influenced by "favoritism," as they often could be in Uganda and many other parts of the world . . .

To which he replied:

My sincere thanks to you Jeanne. In as far as I have not succeeded in get[ting] a scholarship, I still notice and covet your efforts.

I have learnt a very big lesson out of this session and since Success is never ending and failure is never final, this should have been a stepping stone, a teacher that has taught me a very big lesson.

I noticed that selection in the United States is not in any way based on Favoritism like it is here in Uganda but instead principals [sic] and procedure.

I also noticed and learnt that Time is the greatest resource and time once wasted can never be regained. Then I surely have to do it in time come 2013.

I am grateful to David for reinforcing the lessons I keep learning about when my help truly is empowering. In this particular case, there was no question of "fixing" or "doing for," but rather simply a matter of exploring ways to truly be of service.

                ಶ   ಶ   ಶ

A Final Lesson

The Buddha once said: "Teach this triple truth to all: a generous heart, kind speech and a life of service and compassion, are the things which renew humanity." In all that I do, and in the many lessons I have learned and relearned in my teaching and learning *(check my assumptions, listen, build relationships, learn together by doing, build community and respect differences)*, all learned with humility, I have tried to incorporate the Buddha's triple truth, especially in leading a life of service and compassion.

As I practice that life of service, one additional important lesson has been a long time in coming: the lesson of self-care. While the modeling I received was to put others first—always—I have learned that if I do only that, then I am not of much use to others, for I have nothing left to give. As John Calvi says, "Our capacity to love our neighbor is diminished because we don't do such a good job of loving ourselves."[49] I have not always done a very good job of loving myself, of taking care of myself before others, but I am learning to live into the words of Parker Palmer:

---

49. In Catherine Whitmire, *Practicing Peace: A Devotional Walk through the Quaker Tradition* (Notre Dame, ID: Sorin Books, 2007), 35.

Self-care is never a selfish act, it is simply good stewardship of the only gift I have, the gift I was put on earth to offer others. Anytime we can listen to true self, and give it the care it requires, we do so not only for ourselves, but for the many others whose lives we touch.[50]

My gift, of speaking up for children, with hands and heart, eyes and ears, can only be felt if I also "wait upon my gift," *wait* as in being patient with myself, *wait* as in honoring my own needs. It is through my work with the Center for Courage and Renewal that I have learned to practice taking care of my needs—daily—quiet time for reading, writing and walking. Only then can I truly be of service.

He who attempts to act and do things for others or for the world without deepening his own self-understanding, freedom, integrity and capacity to love, will not have anything to give others . . .[51]

I have had to learn to temper my enthusiasm with healthy doses of self-reflection. "Love thy neighbor as thyself," really means just that: *Love thy neighbor—as thyself.*

Only through my own self-understanding do I become a better teacher. We each have a story, and I am shaped by my

---

50. Parker J. Palmer, *Let Your Life Speak* (San Francisco, CA: Jossey-Bass, 2000), 30.

51. Thomas Merton, *Contemplation in a World of Action* (New York: Doubleday, 1971), 164.

story, just as you are shaped by yours. "Everything that happens to you is your teacher," says Polly Berends, "the secret is to learn to sit at the feet of your own life and be taught by it."[52]

The details of my story are important only in how they have shaped me (and therefore, how I am in the world), and hopefully will evoke in you a desire to explore the details of your own life, as we find our commonalities with the human story. If I were to live my life over, I doubt I would have done it much differently, for it has unfolded in unpredictable ways with what I think of as "courageous curiosity," and yet always remained rooted in a sense of purpose and calling to be of service.

How do we become *us*, embracing and appreciating differences, so that we might bring peace to this world? We shall have to start with the children. Perhaps peace will not happen in my lifetime, but it is well worth striving for. In the words of Vaclav Havel, "It is I who must begin. . ."[53]

And I must start with myself, for *I will never stop loving children; I love life too much.*

---

52. Polly Berrien Berends, *Coming to Life: Traveling the Spiritual Path in Everyday Life* (San Francisco, CA: Harper San Francisco, 1990), 8.

53. Vaclav Havel, *Letters to Olga.* Translated by Paul Wilson. (New York, NY: Alfred Knopf, 1988), 54.

After Words

Food for Thought

It is true that we are called to create a better world. But we are first of all called to a more immediate and exalted task: that of creating our own lives.[54]

I do believe we *teach who we are*. I have told my story and how my story informed my teaching, as an invitation for you to tell your story.

Whether you are a teacher, a parent, a therapist, a social worker, or anyone whose calling touches the lives of children, I invite you to explore some of the questions I have asked myself:

☙ What is *the thread I follow*?

---

[54] Thomas Merton, *Love and Living* (New York, NY: Farrar, Strauss Giroux, 1979), 159.

❧ How have I been a good steward for the gift I have been given?

❧ How am I practicing *waiting upon my gift?*

❧ What are the events of my life that make me *fierce with reality?*

❧ How does the *mirror* of my classroom reflect the lives of my students?

❧ How do I *see, hear, understand, and touch* the hearts of my children?

❧ How do I *listen beyond words*—not just with my ears, but with my whole being—to the *belief behind the behavior?*

❧ How do I help a community discover how we all *fit together*, as pieces of a common puzzle, into a world where *we* can become *us?*

❧ How do I honor each *unique manifestation of the human spirit?*

∽ How do I help each child become *more at home on the face of the earth?*

∽ How do I help us all reach through the *holes in the walls that separate us with compassion and connection?*

∽ What can I learn from children, who still have the capacity to believe in the goodness of the human heart?

∽ How do I engage a learner, not just the mind, but also the soul?

∽ How do I open doors as an invitation—not to lead or push or even point the way, unless requested?

∽ Can I take the time to bring relevant curriculum material to my children?

∽ What responsibilities do I have as a parent or an educator to help children continue to question the source of bias?

∽ How do I take care of myself?

ॐ How do I learn to pay attention to my own assumptions?

ॐ How do I cross lines of difference with integrity, grace and humility?

Teaching is about becoming "real" to one another.

Gratitude

To children everywhere, for their realness and the promise of hope. To my sons, Nik and Luke, who continue to be both my teachers and my champions. To my parents, Robbins and Kitty Strong, whose remarkable life stories inspired me to tell my own, and who, even in their passing, taught me about life. To my grandfather, Tracy Strong, who believed in me.

To my many mentors and role models, Barbara McAllister who taught me how to listen to children; Parker Palmer whose wisdom continues to inspire me; Andrea and Alan Rabinowitz for modeling grace and an insatiable curiosity; Jane Kibuuka, for her advocacy for children, her vision and boundless energy, and for teaching me how dreams can come true, even when faced with insurmountable odds.

To Carol Ladas Gaskin, whose simple statement, "there's more to this story..." inspired the writing of this book. To my earliest readers, Sarah Schmidt, Penny Harger, Jennifer Ladd, and others too numerous to name for their supportive feedback. Without their encouragement, this all would have ended up simply a stack of recycled paper on a shelf.

To my editor, A.T. Birmingham-Young, who invited me to show up in my writing, for her unwavering support and enthusiasm. To Sandy Welch, for her patience and the brilliant cover design. To Carrie Wicks, for her eagle-eyed proofreading. To David Trowbridge and my friends at Abiding Nowhere Press, who showed me what is possible. To all the many friends and colleagues along the way, named and unnamed, I am deeply grateful.

Speak Up for a Child

Other books from Abiding Nowhere Press:

Bite into the Day: One Day at a Time, a book of poetry
by Miriam Sonn Raabe

Enso House: Caring for Each Other at the End of Life
by David Daiku Trowbridge

*In Awe of Being Human: A Doctor's Stories from the Edge
of Life and Death,* by Betsy McGregor, M.D.

Abiding Nowhere Press
www.abidingnowhere.com